LINUX FOR BEGINNERS:

an easy and intuitive system to start using linux (basic commands, installation and configuration).

Table of Contents

Description 1

Introduction 5

Chapter 1: Getting started with Linux 7

Chapter 2: Choosing a Linux Distribution System 19

Chapter 3: Connecting to the Internet with Linux 33

Chapter 4: Essential Linux Commands 35

Chapter 5: Linux's Available Features 47

Chapter 6: Disk Storage Management 59

Chapter 7: Redirecting Commands in Linux 77

    Using Redirection 79

Chapter 8: User and Group Management 85

    Users and Groups 85

    Getting Superuser Access 88

    Using Su to Switch Users 90

Chapter 9: Commands and Functions for the Beginner 93

Chapter 10: Using Linux Text Editors 95

    How to Use GUI Text Editors 95

Using ed and vi as Text Editors...96

Chapter 11: Coding with Linux 105

More Linux commands..111

Chapter 12: Programming in Linux using Python............113

Chapter 13: Advanced Shell Programming......................121

Chapter 14: Blockchain, Linux, and Net Neutrality 141

Become a Blockchain Node 148

Become a Blockchain Miner...150

Linux and the Internet of Things (500 words) 152

Chapter 15: Build and Edit Applications.........................155

Use an Integrated Development Environment................................157

Write Patches 158

Conclusion...163

Description

Linux has a long history of change and innovation which turned it into a creative platform for every programming individual that wants to tailor their system to their needs. People often do not come to Linux with words of praise since it is not an uncommon occurrence for a person to give up on Linux based on the first appearance.

The command interface can be a bit overwhelming at first glance. Sometimes it might be hard to remember even the most basic of commands and how they work. However, while it is true that there are loads of commands to memorize, you have many different tools that will lighten your load and help you out immensely with whatever you choose to do with your terminal. You will have to spend some time with getting to know the system, but your learning process will not be as extensive as it seems. If you have an administrator, you have nothing to worry about, as they will take care of most of the problematic occurrences. If this is not the case, the system itself will provide you with much help and, if that is not enough, you can turn to the community which will usually try to support you with their technical knowledge.

Being a relatively old operating system, it is natural to think that Linux's methods will be outdated, but that is not the case. Most Linux distributions are updated regularly and are up to par with most other operating systems in the same category. The many different distros will offer you plenty of options to choose from once you get started. There are even distros that are tailored to the needs of specific groups of individuals. Distros made for designers, distros made for programmers, distros made for office workers—you can find them all. On top of that, no matter which distro you choose, you can make your own customizations, adding tools, applications, and programs.

Several programs that you might need from Windows have been rewritten for Linux, or, more simply and more impressively, the part of the system which garnered said program was rewritten to be compatible with the Linux code. Linux will be able to replace any other operating system to a certain degree. While it might not have the variety of programs and applications or the speed of Windows, it does a good job of emulating it on a budget. While Windows software tends to be updated fairly often, Linux is updated fairly rarely, but the updates are always significant to the system. Linux always tends to match its competitors in whatever possible, which paves a straight and unending road of self-improvement. Linux is always pushed to improve by both the market and the community, as well as the administrators. This means that the quality will mostly be consistent for every distro alike.

This guide will focus on the following:

- Getting started with Linux
- Choosing a Linux Distribution System

- Connecting to the Internet with Linux
- Essential Linux Commands
- Linux's Available Features
- Disk Storage Management
- Redirecting Commands in Linux
- User and Group Management
- Commands and Functions for the Beginner
- Using Linux Text Editors
- Coding with Linux
- Programming in Linux using Python... AND MORE!!!

Introduction

Linux is a highly recommendable piece of software that will fit as many needs of as many individuals as possible. It will learn and grow beside you. While it is a fragile system, it is a work of art in its own right. Countless hours and lines of code were dedicated to make Linux what it is. The kernel itself is an astonishing piece, as it could never have been made by a single man, not only because of the complexity but the amount of work that it would take for one man to do all of that. From a financial standpoint, the creation of the original kernel would have set somebody back several billion. Together with all of the existing distros as well as additional programs, this would eventually turn into a much larger number. This, once again, shows us how Linux is a symbol of unity more than anything. So many people in the world, connected by nothing more than the fact that they want to create something that will be of use to everyone, converge together time and time again to elevate the quality of the operating system to newer and newer heights. The original idea of the Linux was an ambitious one indeed, but it could never have hoped to reach what it has now.

Many skeptics are quick to dismiss Linux, comparing it to larger, more influential systems like Windows and macOS saying that it is slower and uglier. They also like to say that it is not user-friendly and hard to use by even those that have the most programming prowess. While it is true that Linux is inferior to many other systems in terms of visual appeal and ease of usage, the point of Linux was never that. While many other operating systems flood you with flashy options and applications, Linux chooses to remain straightforward in its approach and deliver results with the utmost simplicity. Linux was made so that people could learn more about the more advanced spheres of programing relatively easily and has been doing the job for many long years. What sets Linux apart from the other operating systems is how truly unique it is in most ways. It is a community-wide effort, so there are no sharks in play who want to prosper on the sweat of others. Everybody does as much as they want to, and we all have the same resources at our disposal. What makes your Linux system different from any other is how you choose to use it. The system is highly intuitive, though a bit hard to master, but being good at anything takes hard work and dedication. Taking care of the system is not an issue either. The commands that are used for this are all highly intuitive and very accurate, which means that you will rarely need the help of a professional when it comes to maintenance, even with huge server systems. There is really nothing bad that can be said about Linux that isn't balanced out by something else. With the amount of steady progress Linux has been making, it is starting to become fiery competition for OSs made by more prominent companies.

Chapter 1: Getting started with Linux

As for the preparation of disk space, this is the most crucial moment in the whole process of installing Linux. The fact is that if you install the system on a computer whose hard disk already has any data, then it is here that you should be careful not to accidentally lose it. If you install a Linux system on a "clean" computer or at least on a new hard disk, where there is no data, then everything is much simpler.

Why can't you install Linux in the same partition where you already have, for example, Windows, even with enough free space?

The fact is that Windows uses the FAT32 file system (in old versions – FAT16) or NTFS (in Windows NT / 2000), and in Linux, a completely different system called Extended File System 2 (ext2fs, in the newest versions – journaling extSfs). These file systems can be located only on different partitions of the hard disk.

Note that in Linux, physical hard disks are referred to as the first is hda, the second is hdb, the third is hdc, and so on (hdd, hde, hdf...).

Sometimes in the installation program of the system you can see the full names of the disks - / dev / hda instead of hda, / dev / hdb instead of hdb, and so on – this is the same thing for us now. The logical partitions of each disk are numbered. So, on a hda physical disk, there are hda1, hda2, and so on, hdb can be hdb1, hdb2, and so on. Do not be confused by the fact that these figures sometimes go in a row. It does not matter to us.

How to start installing Linux from disk

To begin installing Linux, insert the system CD into the drive and restart the computer by selecting the boot from CD. If you plan to install Linux over Windows, then the installation program can be run directly from it.

Moreover, if you are running Windows 95/98, the installation will start immediately, and if the installation program was launched from under a more powerful system, for example, Windows 2000, XP, Vista, Seven will still have to restart the computer from the CD disk.

Your computer may already be configured to boot from a CD. If the boot from the CD does not occur, when you restart your computer, enter the BIOS settings. On most systems, to do this, immediately after turning on the computer or restarting, press the Delete key or F11.

Enter it by first moving the pointer to it using the cursor keys and then pressing the Enter key. Now find in the parameters either the item Boot Sequence (boot order), or, if not, the item 1st boot device (first boot device). Use the cursor keys to select the desired item and, by changing its value using the Page Up and Page Down keys, make the first bootable CD-ROM device. Most likely, the computer will ask you to confirm this intention. Usually, to confirm, you must press the Y key, which means yes.

All modern computers can boot from a CD. If for some reason your computer does not have this capability, you will have to create a boot diskette to install Linux. There are always special tools for this on the Linux distribution CD.

Usually, they are located in a folder called dos tools (or in a folder with a similar name). There are images of boot floppies and a DOS program for creating them. Read the README files on the distribution CD for more detailed instructions.

The installation of the Linux operating system can be divided into several stages:

• DISK SPACE PREPARATION;

• SELECTION OF THE PROGRAMS (PACKAGES) YOU NEED;

• DEVICE CONFIGURATION AND GRAPHICAL INTERFACE;

• INSTALL BOOTLOADER.

The installation program takes control of the entire process. You should only answer questions if the installation does not occur in fully automatic mode.

How to install Linux from a flash drive?

It often happens that if you want to install the OS, a person is faced with the fact that his drive is broken or missing. Especially often this problem happens with laptop owners. But do not be upset, because there is an alternative: installing from a Linux flash drive. To do this, you do not need a great deal of knowledge in programming, because there are special programs that "burn" the Linux image onto your USB flash drive just like on a disk. You will only need to start the installation process.

So, before you install Linux from a flash drive, you will need a flash drive with an image written onto it.

First, you should prepare the BIOS for installation.

As an example, consider installing a Linux Mint distribution. For the installation of Linux Mint from a flash drive to begin, you need to configure the startup parameters.

We insert the USB flash drive into the computer, turn it on at the very beginning, when there is a black screen on the screen and a lot of text, press the F2 button. Depending on the version of the BIOS and the computer, it may be another button – F10, Delete or Esc.

We get into the settings menu and now we need to find the "Boot" item. Again, in different versions of the BIOS it may be called differently but be guided by this word. After we have found the autorun menu, a list of priorities appears before our eyes. It contains: a hard disk, a disk drive, a removable hard disk, USB inputs, and so on. Our task is to find a flash drive in this list and put it in priority for 1 place.

It is done this way: we point the arrows at the name (for example: "USB 40GB DEVICE") and move it by pressing the F5 and F6 buttons until the USB flash drive is in 1st place.

Now the system will start the flash drive first. Press F10 and confirm the output by entering the Y (Yes) key and pressing the Enter button.

Reboot the computer.

After that you should start the installation process.

After the computer restarts, you will see the startup menu. Often it is decorated with various images, so you will understand exactly what it is. Press Enter.

If nothing has changed or something went wrong, restart your computer and read the menu list for details. It is possible that not only the Linux installation, but also various programs are present on the recorded image.

Then you should Install it from a Linux flash drive.

All the torment behind! Already at the beginning of the installation, you will be greeted by a friendly Russian-language interface. Start by choosing a language. Select your preferred language.

Next, you need to make sure that the computer has enough free hard disk space, is connected to a power source, and is connected to the Internet. You can immediately agree that the latest updates are automatically downloaded during installation.

Click "Next." We get into the hard disk selection menu. In it, you can format and split partitions, if desired. Specify the partition (disk) in which you want to install the operating system and click the "Install Now" button.

Here you can increase the amount of memory, change the file system type, format the partition and specify the mount point. Use the "Ext4" file system and set the mount point "/". If there is no valuable information on the hard disk, it is advisable to format the partition. Click "Install Now".

Now we select the country and city of residence so that the system automatically sets the time and other indicators for your personal needs. Also, specify the keyboard layout. It remains to enter the desired name for your computer, a name for the user and a password (optional). Click "Next" and start the installation process.

After the installation is complete, restart the computer, remove the USB flash drive and wait for the Linux operating system to start.

How to make a bootable USB flash drive for Linux

Today, the operating system is becoming increasingly popular. Surely you have already heard from your friends or acquaintances stories about how easy it is to carry out such an installation. Obviously, creating a bootable USB flash drive for Linux is a great way to reinstall the operating system on a computer with a damaged or missing drive, laptop, or netbook. Let's get acquainted with this installation method better!

First, you need to find and download a Linux operating system image.

Finding images of different versions of Linux on the Internet is very simple because it is "freeware" and is distributed absolutely free. Download the desired image on our website, official website or torrents.

A bootable Linux flash drive requires a regular flash drive. Its volume should be 1GB and higher.

Next you need to download the program Unetbootin.

This program will help us with how to make a bootable Linux flash drive. You can download it from the page unetbootin.sourceforge.net. At the top of the site there are buttons for 3 distributions – Windows, Linux and Mac OS. If you, for example, now have Windows, then press the Windows button.

After downloading, the program opens instantly, and you do not need to install it. If you have problems with the launch (Windows 7), run "on behalf of the administrator."

Initially, the program is ticked on the "Distribution", but we need to put it on the "Disk Image". We also indicate that this is an ISO image. Next, click on the button "..." and select the image that we previously downloaded from the Internet.

If your flash drive is capacious enough, then it is advisable to allocate space in the file storage space. 100 MB will be enough.

And at the very bottom of the program window, select which flash drive you want to burn. Example – "Type: USB drive; Media: E: \ ". If only one flash drive is inserted into the computer, the program will determine it on its own and there is no need to choose anything.

It remains only to press the "OK" button and wait until the program completes the burning of the image. It takes 5-10 minutes.

That is all you need to know about how to burn Linux to a USB flash drive. After burning, you must restart the computer or insert the USB flash drive into the computer where you want to install the Linux Operating System.

How to choose programs to install

So, the most crucial moment – the layout of the hard drive – is behind. Now the installation program proceeds to the next stage, in which it will offer to select the necessary programs (packages are traditionally called programs in Linux, which, by the way, is truer in terms of terminology).

You can simply choose one of the options for installing packages (for home computer, office, workstation with a connection to a local network, etc.). Alternatively, by turning on the Package selection switch manually, go to the software package selection window.

If it is not clear from the name of the program what it is for, click on the name, and a brief description of the purpose of this program will appear in a special window. Unfortunately, in Russian-language distributions, often not all descriptions are translated into Russian, so some descriptions may be in English.

Having chosen the necessary packages for installation, be sure to locate on the screen and check the box to check dependencies. The fact is that some programs may depend on others, that is, they may use modules of other programs in their work.

Some programs may require the presence of any other software packages for normal operation. In this case, they say that one program depends on another. For example, the kreatecd CD burning program contains only a graphical user interface and calls the cdrecord console program for the actual recording, although the user doesn't see it when working.

This means that the kreatecd program depends on cdrecord. When installing Linux, all software dependencies are checked automatically; you just need to allow the installation program to do this by turning on the appropriate switch.

The checkbox for checking dependencies is needed for the installer to automatically check if some of the selected programs are using those packages that are not selected for installation. Having made such a check, the installation program will provide you with a list of these packages and will offer to install them as well. We should agree with this, otherwise, some programs will not work.

Configure devices and graphical interface

After you agree to install the necessary packages, the process of copying the necessary files to the hard disk will begin. This process is quite long, so you can go and drink coffee at this time, for at least five to ten minutes. However, if your distribution is recorded on two or more compact discs, the installer will from time to time ask you to insert the necessary compact disc into the drive.

Then the configuration of additional devices and the graphical interface will begin. There is one subtlety. The fact is that most installation programs for some reason incorrectly process information about the mouse. Therefore, the question of what kind of mouse you have at this stage is to answer a simple two-button or a simple three-button. Do not look in the list of the manufacturer, model, and so on.

After installing the system, it will be possible to separately enable additional functions of the mouse (for example, the operation of the scroll wheel) if they do not work themselves.

Install the bootloader

After all the above operations, the freshly installed system is ready for operation. However, the installer will ask you to answer one more question: should the boot loader be installed and, in most cases, if necessary, which one?

If Linux is the only operating system on your computer, then you will not need a bootloader. In this case, simply restart the computer, removing the bootable CD from it.

If you specifically changed the BIOS settings in order to allow the computer to boot from a CD or from a floppy disk, then now, after installing the system, you can reconfigure the computer to boot only from the hard disk. To do this, go back to the BIOS settings and change the boot order. However, if you specified the "universal" boot order – Floppy, CDROM, IDEO – you can no longer change it, just make sure that when you turn on and restart your computer, no boot diskettes or a CD are inserted in it, unless necessary boot from these devices.

Chapter 2: Choosing a Linux Distribution System

Which distribution should you choose?

Finding the distribution that suits your needs will depend on the answers to the following questions:

• How experienced are you in using computers?

• What do you like – traditional or a modern desktop interface?

• Desktop or a server?

In case you possess average skills in using computers, then the latest and user-friendly distributions like Deepin, Ubuntu, and Linux Mint is the best choice. Fedora or Debian is the best option for all of those who possess above average computer skills. The distribution Gentoo is for all of the people who have mastered computers and are knowledgable about the system administration.

Are you looking out for a server-only distribution? If that is the case, then you will have to decide whether you want only the desktop interface or would like to do it with the help of the command line. GUI interfaces are not installed on the Ubuntu server. It means that you need to have a strong understanding of

Linux operating system. Using a command of Sudo apt-get install ubuntu-desktop, you can install the GUI on the Ubuntu Server. Would you prefer a distribution that would offer you everything that you require for the server? CentOS is the perfect choice for such a case. Or, do you prefer a desktop distribution and then add on things as you like and need? Ubuntu Linux or Debain can be the right choice.

Following is the list of features the best Linux distributions have for new users:

User-friendly

This is one point where our debate can last forever. Thus, what should be done is, a new user should choose a distribution and start using it without a lot of explanation. In case there is a need to provide a detailed explanation, the distribution is certainly not user-friendly. For instance, any person without any coaching can start using the Windows 7 desktop. It is something every Linux desktop should consider.

App store

People are now getting too dependent on the mobile version, and they need to become accustomed to the app store on their home computer as well.

Applications

The basic necessities should be pre-installed, and users should not need to install them separately. So what are the necessities at present, as they keep changing often?

- Email

- *Music player*

- *Office Suite*

- *We browser*

The list of applications to be installed depends on a person's needs.

Modern interface

There are many plenty attractive mobile landscapes, and thus, the desktop now needs to draw user's attention with a modern, unique and simple interface.

Ubuntu, Linux Mint, and Linux Deepin are the most commonly preferred distributions and following, is the ranking given to each of them according to the features:

User-friendliness

Rank 1 - Linux Mint

Rank 2 - Ubuntu Linux

Rank 3 - Linux Deepin

App store

Rank 1- Linux Deepin

Rank 2 - Linux Mint

Rank 3 - Ubuntu Linux

Applications

Rank 1- Linux Mint

Rank 2 - Ubuntu Linux

Rank 3 - Linux Deepin

Modern Interface

Rank 1- Linux Deepin

Rank 2 - Ubuntu Linux

Rank 3 - Linux Mint

According to your preferences and needs, you can choose the Linux distribution.

Where to obtain Linux Distribution

Along with providing a professional- level and stable Linux systems, the distributions provide the KDE and GNOME interfaces, hassle free and easy to use configuration tools, a variety of Internet services, an array of multimedia applications, and countless Linux applications of different types. Information about different distributions can be found at their respective websites. CDs and DVDs can be downloaded from these sites which can then be used to install Linux. Some distributions even provide live CDs which can be run on the CD-ROM drive and you would not need to install it on your hard drive.

Distribution supported repositories also provide most of the software from the major distributions. They are available for downloading. Install disk images are available as both smaller desktop-only installs and large serve installs. Live-CD can be used to install Linux if provided.

The strategy for distribution includes the install disks and collection of software which can later be updated from the complete and diverse list of software on the distribution repositories. It means that you can start with the selection of software at a relatively smaller level. All the installations will have to undergo a constant update.

It is mandatory to read all the instructions for the distribution you're downloading. These can be found online on the website of the distribution and can be accessed through any browser.

What Defines a Linux Distribution?

Linux distribution is just not about the look and feel, but a lot of different things goes into making a distribution. While you're searching for the right distribution, you should take all those things into consideration. Most of these things can be installed separately, like if you don't like the apps or desktop environments of a particular distribution, you can install them individually. The idea of finding the right distribution means that you can find something that meets your ideal setup. You'll be spending less time and energy if you follow this approach. Here are some of the important points which you should keep in mind while choosing the distribution.

Package Managers

Package Manager or Package Management system helps you in maintaining the installation, upgradation, configuration and removal of computer programs consistently with the presence of a collection of software tools. It is one of the biggest features that differentiates various distributions. APT is the package manager for Ubuntu, and the same system is available on other distributions like Mint, Debian, etc. However, some distributions have their own package managers. Yum manager (Fedora) for instance is easier to use through command line as compared to APT. It can be slower at times, though.

Where ease of use matters, the availability of a particular package manager should also be kept in mind. Fedora is not as popular as other distribution using APT so it can be difficult for you to find the exact app you're looking for. You'll have to build it from sources instead of getting it directly through repositories. While it is easier to build from sources, you'll get stuck when you are not able to update when a new version is released automatically. So, you have to take into account both the ease of use and accessibility of the package manager.

Desktop Environment

We have already seen different desktop environments, their differences and how they are important to the overall working of the Linux system. While choosing the right distribution, the desktop environment should be kept in mind. Some of the important things about desktop environments can be recalled here to understand how it affects your choice for the right distribution.

These includes things like:

• The overall look and feel of your windows, menus and desktop and its overall customizability.

• The usage of resource

• Different options available in your distribution's graphical preferences (like changing the items you want to appear in your menus or remapping of certain keys).

• The overall integration of different programs with your desktop.

Although a separate desktop environment can be installed, no one can deny its importance while choosing the distribution. You will save time if the default desktop environment is close to what you want, you'll not have to install it separately. It will also work in a better with the rest of the programs.

Stability vs. Cutting Edge

Distributions have a specific release and update cycles. While some keep updating and provide the most up to date version of apps and packages, others delay the upgrade process to ensure stability. Fedora, provides the latest and greatest by giving the most up to date versions, whereas Debian, will intentionally delay the release of certain updates to make everything is running smoothly. So you have the option of choosing according to your preference. You can go for Fedora if you enjoy the latest versions of Firefox or any other app. If stability is your priority, then sticking to Debian would be the best option.

Hardware Compatibility

Different distributions package drivers differently, this is to say that the printer compatibility will depend on the distribution you choose. Some printers might work for one distribution, but not for another. Although, you can install drivers separately for your printer, you can save time and effort by finding a distribution that supports your printer. Other things like Wi-Fi, sound, and video cards should be checked for compatibility from the hardware compatibility pages of the distribution. If you find it there, then you are good to go or else you will have to put a little extra to install drivers.

Community Support

Community Support has become an important aspect in my fields today. Finding the right answers easily through these forums can solve your problem, and you no longer have to be annoyed at issues which you can't resolve by yourself. Linux is no different, and community support is a big help for Linux users. While choosing the right distribution, you should check the community surrounding it. Troubleshooting help, app support, or even generic information is essential for beginners. It is this one aspect that has made Ubuntu a popular choice as a distribution. You can search for different forums for distributions and choose the one you find most helpful and providing the best support.

The Must-Use Distributions

After discovering the factors which constitute in your choice for the distribution, the next step is exploring the options. 'DistroWatch' is an excellent resource to find different distributions. The number of distributions is in hundreds so you can find the information overwhelming. Below is the list compiled of some of the most popular distributions, but you can feel free to explore other options. Although these distributions offer a variation of the desktop environment, we will stick to the default one to make it simple.

Ubuntu (Standard)

Ubuntu is a great distribution for beginners. It is made with an aim to make Linux easier to use for average person – which it has fulfilled. It is updated every six months and extremely easy to use. It has its own Unity interface which offers unique features like dock instead of a taskbar, and the package manager is in the form of an App Store like the interface and a dashboard which makes searching process easier. Although most of the people like it, you always have the option to bring it back to the GNOME interface if you like. The standard apps which come with Ubuntu include Firefox, Empathy (instant messaging), Thunderbird, and other apps like Transmission for downloading torrents. You won't have to build from source as Ububtu has a great hardware compatibility. The community support for Ububtu is the best, so if you're looking for a hassle-free option, Ububtu should be your pick.

Linux Mint (Made for beginners)

Although Linux Mint is based on Ububtu, it has gained popularity separately, especially after the introduction of the Unity interface by Ububtu. The purpose of Mint Linux is to make the process as simple as possible for people who are not familiar with Linux. The menus are easy to use, and the installation process is hassle-free. Many applications like Adobe Flash, MP3 support, and other hardware drivers come preinstalled, and you don't have to install them separately like you have to do for other distributions. The default or preinstalled apps are similar to that of Ubuntu (with Pidgin taking the place of Empathy for instant messaging). The package manager followed is the same as Ububtu, which gives you the ease of access to different programs available in repositories. The community support is extensive as novice mostly use this distribution. Linux Mint is highly recommended if you've never used Linux before.

Fedora (Bleeding Edge User)

Fedora is known for its up to date and cutting edge software. The updates usually come out after six months, as is the case with Ubuntu, but unlike Ubuntu, those updates are not supported for a longer period. The users are expected to update as soon as possible. If Mozilla releases an update for Firefox, the programs will be updated immediately in Fedora, while Ubuntu makes specific changes to the program before releasing the update. This consistent update can result in some instability, but people who always prefer the latest version don't care much about this. It is the most popular Linux distribution which can be easily updated to GNOME. Ubuntu and Mint's ATP is somewhat harder to use as compared to the slow, but easier to use Yum package manager. The software availability is not as extensive as that found in Ubuntu or Mint, and you can still get most of the software through repositories. The enterprise and security features of Fedora makes it popular for use in the professional environment. Serious Linux users will definitely prefer Fedora.

Debian (Cautious and Stable)

Debian is opposite to Fedora in many ways. Its aim is to remain as stable as possible – which it does adeptly. The downside is that your system is not up to date, most of the times. The new releases come out after 1 to 3 years, but if you don't care much about having the latest version, and are content with stability, Debian is the right pick for you. The package management system used by Debian is the same as that of Ubuntu and Mint, which means that you will get most of the programs, and you don't have to checkout repositories. If you have an old or offbeat build, you're going to like Debian as it supports many processor architectures.

OpenSUSE (Made for Tinkerer)

OpenSUSE has a really helpful community and a general purpose Linux distribution. The level of configuration it offers makes it stand out from other distributions. While KDE is the default desktop, you get the option of choosing from different desktops like KDE, GNOME, XFCE and LXDE while you're installing. The added benefits of OpenSUSE is a good system administration utility and package manager (YaST) and the ease of access to documentation through the community. Opting KDE and OpenSUSE means that it can be resource heavy, so you need to make sure that you have sufficient resources before making the decision. If you want to have the freedom of choice, you can get it by choosing OpenSUSE as it offers many configuration options, and you wouldn't have to delve into the command line.

Arch Linux (For the Adamant)

Arch Linux requires you to start from scratch. It doesn't have many characteristics of its own, and you make everything, by yourself. All you have when you start is the command line. From this, you build your desktop environment, applications you prefer, drivers and all other things you need along the way. You're making a customized distribution of Arch Linux. It takes a lot of work and effort but the result is what's important for you. You will learn a great deal through the process. It is a great learning experience as you will be able to figure out in case something went wrong (with the help of the community, it is usually really helpful).

The 'Pacman' package manager is used by Arch which is extremely powerful. You are always up to date with the last versions. Arch User Repository (AUR) is a great platform where installable versions of all the programs are built by the community. Although it is not an official platform, you can get to install all the programs you might need with AUR helper, just like normal packages in the repositories.

There are many other Linux distributions as well like Slackware or CentOS. There are also variations of these basic distributions like LXDE-enabled Lubuntu (which is based on Ubuntu as the name suggests). You can start with the basic ones but is recommended that you try different distributions as it will only help you learn a lot about Linux, but you would understand your needs in a better way.

Chapter 3: Connecting to the Internet with Linux

Connection to the Internet is carried out using a physical channel between your computer and the provider's server.

There are three main methods for organizing a physical connection:

- WIRELESS NETWORK;

- THE LOCAL NETWORK;

- A MODEM THROUGH WHICH PPP IS EXCHANGED.

In the first case, a wireless access point is required. Only if available is it possible to set up a wireless network with the Internet.

The second method is used when your computer is connected to a local network, in which there is a server for access to the world wide web. In this case, you do not need to put your efforts into the organization of the connection – the local network administrator will do all that is necessary for you. Just launch a browser, enter the URL you are interested in, and access it.

And the third way is a dial-up modem connection. In this case, the administrator will not help you, so you have to do everything yourself. For these reasons, we decided to consider this method in more detail.

First, naturally, you should have a modem and a telephone. Next, you need to decide on the provider that provides access to the Internet and get from it the phone number by which your PC will connect to the modem pool of the provider and, of course, your username and password to access the global network.

Next, you need to configure the PPP protocol. This can be done manually, or you can use the configuration program. Manual configuration is quite complicated and requires editing files and writing scripts. Therefore, it is preferable for beginners to work with a special program that automates the entire process of setting up access to the Internet.

This program is called kppp and is originally included in the KDE graphical environment. This utility makes it much easier to set up a connection and, in most cases, requires you to only correctly specify accounting information.

Chapter 4: Essential Linux Commands

In this chapter we explain basic Linux commands that will help you to deal with files and directories, text processing commands, users and groups, process management, networks, and the help system.

Files and Directories

touch

The *touch* command is used to update the access date or modification date of a file and works in two ways: if the file already exists, the timestamp for access and modification of the file is set to the current timestamp. In case the file does not exist yet, an empty file will be created that has the current timestamp (see image below).

Use the touch command in order to set the timestamp of a file and to figure out if you have the appropriate permissions to write to a directory or an entire filesystem.

ls

This command lists the entries of a directory. The image below shows two common ways: without any options, and with the options -*la* (short for -l -a which means long all). The first output displays the entry names only for regular files, whereas the second output lists both regular and hidden entries. Over and above, it shows all the information like type of entry, permissions, name of owner, size of entry, access date and name of entry.

In order to list directories only, use the option -*d* (abbreviates -- directory).

mkdir

This command is used in order to create a directory (make directory). The following example creates a new directory named "training" in the current directory:

```
$ mkdir training

$
```

rmdir

This command is used in order to remove an empty directory (remove directory). The following example deletes an empty directory named "training" in the current directory.

```
$ rmdir training

$
```

rm

This command abbreviates the word "remove" and deletes files and directories. In order to delete all the files ending with .*txt* that reside in the current directory issue the following command:

```
$ rm *.txt

$
```

In order to be on the safe side when deleting files and directories, use the option -*i* (or --interactive) in combination with -*v* (for --verbose). Before deleting a file *rm* will then request your explicit confirmation, and prints a status message:

```
$ rm -iv invoice156.txt

rm: remove regular file "invoice156.txt"? y

"invoice156.txt" was deleted

$
```

cp

The *cp* command copies files. In order to operate properly, it requires two names: the name of the original file and the name of the copy. The next example creates a copy of the calendar file that is named "calendar-2018".

```
$ cp calendar calendar-2018

$
```

The original file is not touched and stays intact. The copy has the same content as the original, but with the current timestamp. Use the option -i (or --interactive) to prevent overwriting existing files.

mv

The *mv* command abbreviates the word "move" and moves and renames files and directories. It requires two names: the name of the original file and its new name. The following example renames the "calendar" file to "calendar-2018".

```
$ mv calendar calendar-2018
$
```

The original file is removed and the new entry receives the current timestamp. Use the option -i (or --interactive) to prevent overwriting existing files.

cd

The *cd* (change directory) command allows you to move through the system. To move into the subdirectory "work", use this command:

```
$ cd work
$
```

file

The *file* command determines the type of entry in the file system. There are three sets of tests that are performed in the following order: filesystem tests, magic tests, and language tests. The first test that succeeds causes the file type to be printed. As shown in the image below "Music" is classified as a directory, "testfile" as an empty file and "/etc/passwd" as a text file. This command also detects PDF files as well as various image formats.

du and df

These two very similar commands tell you more about the disk space that is in use, *du* abbreviates "disk usage" and *df* means "disk free".

du calculates the amount of disk space that is used by a directory. The regular output states the value for every single entry and can be a bit confusing. In order to get a summary for a directory, extend the command line call by the three parameters *-s*, *-c* and *-h*. *-s* abbreviates "summary", *-c* means "total" and *-h* outputs the value in human-readable format. The image below shows the disk usage of your home directory.

In contrast, the *df* command shows how much space is left on the devices. The image below shows the available disk space of your system. From left to right the columns cover the filesystem, the disk size, the amount of space that is used, the amount of space that is still available and the device that is mounted to that directory.

Output and Text Processing

echo

echo is a built-in shell command and is intended to output text:

```
$ echo help

help
$
```

The next example prints the value of the shell variable *$HOME* which represents your home directory.

```
$ echo $HOME

/home/user
$
```

cat and tac

These two commands print a file, line by line. *cat* starts with the first line up to the last line, and *tac* starts with the last line up to the first line. The next example uses a simple plain text file named "places" that contains the names of one city per line. For *cat* Amsterdam comes first, and for *tac* it is Cape Town.

```
$ cat places

Amsterdam
Berlin
Bern
Cape Town

$ tac places

Cape Town

Bern
Berlin
Amsterdam
$
```

grep

This command abbreviates the description "global regular expression print". The command acts as a filter that only prints the lines of text that match a given pattern. *grep* needs data to work on, in combination with a pattern to look for.

Based on the example used above for *cat* and *tac*, the following command line call only outputs the lines from the file that contain the character string "Ber". Keep in mind that *grep* filters are case-sensitive, i.e. it looks for the character string that starts with an uppercase "B" followed by the two lowercase letters "e" and "r". It does not matter whether the pattern is at the beginning, in the middle or at the end of text.

```
$ grep Ber places

Berlin
Bern
$
```

When it comes to patterns, *grep* supports character strings and regular expressions (RegEx). In order to find all the strings that end with the letter "n" use the option *-E* (or --extended-regexp) followed by the pattern "n$" as shown below:

```
$ grep -E "n$" places

Berlin
Bern
Cape Town

$
```

head and tail

head outputs the first lines from a file. Invoked without further parameters it outputs up to ten lines. In contrast *tail* does the same thing, but starts at the end of a file. In order to output the first two lines, add the option *-n 2* as follows:

```
$ head -n 2 places

Amsterdam
Berlin
$
```

In order to output the last two lines, do the same thing using *tail* as follows. In contrast to *tac* (*tail* does not change the order of output.

```
$ tail -n 2 places

Bern
Cape Town

$
```

nl

nl is similar to *cat* but adds a line number at the beginning of each line of output.

```
$ nl places

    1 Amsterdam

    2 Berlin

    3 Bern
```

```
    4 Cape Town

$
```

wc

This command abbreviates the phrase "word count" and counts lines, words and single characters of the input data. Unless otherwise specified, all three values are printed:

```
$ wc places

4  5 32 places

$
```

Amongst others *wc* offers the following options to limit the output:

- -l: output the number of lines only, followed by the filename

- -w: output the number of words only, followed by the filename

- -c: output the number of characters only, followed by the filename

This example shows how to count only the lines in a file:

```
$ wc -l places

4 places

$
```

Users and Groups

These commands deal with a variety of actions in order to manage the users and groups of your Linux system. Unless explicitly stated, these commands can be run as a regular user.

whoami

This command returns your current user ID as follows:

```
$ whoami

user
$
```

Chapter 5: Linux's Available Features

The advantages of Linux are found within the kernel. By understanding the Linux kernel, you can modify the operating system to include support for the features you want. Many people have altered the kernel specifically for their needs in the past, and these features have become an integral part of many Linux distributions.

Multiuser

While you can have multiple users with Windows, you lack the ability to have those multiple users logged on at the same time. This means you are limited in how many people can be working on the system at once. With Linux, multiple users can work on the system at the same time, and each user can customize their working environment to suit their own needs.

Each user has their own unique directory where files are stored, desktop with icons, menus, and applications. You are, of course, able to password protect these accounts in order to protect your applications and data, and control who is able to access them, even on the same system.

Hardware Support

There are a number of support options available for the hardware connected to computer. This involves anything from floppy disk drives (if you still have them), CDs, DVDs, USBs, sound cards, external tape devices, and basically anything else that is compatible with a computer system.

However, the Linux community will often write a driver to be compatible with your distribution within a short amount of time.

Application Support

Due to the fact that Linux is compatible with POSIX, as well as a number of other application programming interfaces (or APIs), there is an immense variety of freeware and shareware software available for Linux. While it may take some streamlining and adjusting, you will be able to run most of the GNU software offered by the Free Software Foundation.

For this reason, the features of Linux are virtually limitless in their functionality. If you need Linux to perform a specific function, you can alter the software and even create your own distribution. While not everyone has this kind of skill, it is possible, and even likely, that the feature you are looking for is available for download.

No Spyware

Spyware has become a massive problem for many Windows users. As soon as a program is downloaded that includes spyware, it begins working. The user may be completely unaware that there are applications running in the background that are collecting user information and sending it back to third parties who use this data to potentially steal their identities or sell the information to marketing companies. These applications can also change the way the computer interprets information. Even better, there is no need to spend money on purchasing and upgrading anti-virus software or paying for costly system recovery.

No Defragmentation

Linux has a very advanced and efficient filing system which does not require the data to be defragmented. In the case of regular Windows computers, these file systems can become fragmented which can cause crashes, slowdowns, and memory loss on your system.

No Crashes

If you have a Windows computer, you are no stranger to random crashes for which you are never given a reason. For example, if you were running Windows and your browser crashed, the entire operating system could come crashing down due to the fact that the system is connected to the Graphic User Interface. This has happened to virtually every Windows user and can be incredibly frustrating when it comes to losing data or interrupting an important task. You will experience none of these crashes with Linux because the Linux core operating system (the kernel) is separated from the Graphic User Interface in the X Window, and from the applications that you use such as OpenOffice.org. If an application were to crash for whatever reason, such as a corrupted file, the core operating system would remain operational.

No Frequent Re-Installation

You will notice that one of the ideal solutions for issues with Windows is to simply reinstall the entire operating system and start from scratch. This can be difficult when it comes to the times that Windows crashes and there is no way to recover the data you have lost. If you run a business using your system, this can be incredibly costly and damaging to your business operations. Linux, on the other hand, will not crash in the same way, meaning your data is safe and recoverable if you are faced with any issues, which are, when it comes to Linux, few and far between. You are actually able to store your data separately from the operating system so that any personal user preferences are able to be stored even if you do choose to reinstall the operating system. This can be done by creating a new partition which will keep your home directory. Similarly, through Windows, you are constantly required to restart the system if any changes are made, such as installing new hardware or software, in order to reconfigure the system. In the case of Linux, there is no need for this.

Many Filing Systems

Windows comes with two filing systems. Linux, on the other hand, brings with it hundreds of filing systems, which is useful for those users who are required to work across multiple computers, exchanging hardware from one system to another.

Powerful Command Line

We have explored some of the basics of using the command line, or the shell environment. With Windows, there is not much farther you can go with the command line, especially for basic users. With Linux's command line, you can write entire programs for Linux, which means that you can eliminate repetitive tasks through automation. An example of this would be backing up your system. This is usually an extremely arduous task; imagine if you could just run a simple program that runs through the entire process with just one click. This and numerous other simplifications are all possible with the Linux command line.

Vendor Independence

With Windows, you are locked into a single vendor if you want to keep your system up-to-date. This can a disincentive for many people who don't want to keep spending money to keep their system safe. With Linux, you are never locked into a single vendor because the community offers a large variety of vendors who each have their own distributions to offer and to provide support for. If you feel that a particular vendor has let you down when it comes to support or if you have encountered a distribution that didn't live up to your expectations, you can either turn to the community for further support or adopt a new vendor altogether. You don't have to start over from scratch or feel trapped with a vendor that doesn't seem to have your best interests in mind. Even better, if a vendor happens to walk away from their distribution, you are not forced to choose a new vendor or distribution, but can instead turn to the ever-growing community to continue publishing your distribution. Keep in mind there are no licensing agreements involved when it comes to Linux, meaning you are free to download, modify, and repackage as you wish.

No Registry

If you have used registry on Windows, you will know that it can be a nightmare. Not only do you need specific tools to open and modify the files, if any of the data is corrupted, it can be extremely frustrating to manage. With Linux, most of the configuration is stored in plain text files. This allows you to easily manage, backup, and transfer these files between systems. This is much simpler than using registry.

High Degree of Documentation

Have you ever had an issue that you simply could not find a solution for? You look through the manual only to come up empty-handed, you search through forums and search engines looking for an answer, but there is just no record of anyone else having the same issue. This is hardly ever the case for problems with Linux. Linux is one of the most documented operating systems and almost all of these documents are free of charge. The documents are not PDFs thrown together by just anyone, but are well-written documents which detail many of the concepts that help explain the inner-working of Linux. This is perhaps one of the greatest advantages to the Linux community, which is comprised of a number of online forums, articles, and groups that are located in virtually every country, city, and town. This means that you are never very far from another Linux user in the case that you would like to have someone help you out with the systems workings in person.

You will find that the community almost behaves like a family since everyone has the same goals and objectives when it comes to improving and developing the open source operating system. The best Linux experience is unlocked when you get involved in this community and offer value to other members, who will surely return the favor.

Package Management

The excellent package management offered by Linux allows users to access tools which can simplify the process of installing and upgrading applications. In addition to this, if you were to upgrade your current distribution of Linux, this is really quite simple. Furthermore, if you are a developer, you have access to a wide range of development tools, libraries, and compilers which come along with the package. For those who are Java developers or Web developers who use PHP/Perl/Ruby or C and C++ coding, you can put your skills to good when using Linux. This gives developers the freedom to use Linux as they wish and even offer and share their own versions of Linux with the community, their friends, and their family.

No Open Ports

One major issue with Windows computers is the fact that unused ports are left open. This can lead to attacks by hackers that can disable and take control of your computer to either inflict harm on your system or carry out further attacks using your computer as a kind of attack zombie. Linux leaves no open ports, which means your data is highly secure and protected from unauthorized entry.

Faster Release Cycle

The patches that are created for Linux distributions are written within hours rather than days or weeks in the case of other operating systems. This means if there is a known issue or threat to the security of your system, patches, which offer protection, will be created much faster than in the case of proprietary software. Additionally, many of the Linux distributions are set to be released every 6 months, making it easy to gain access to the latest application updates, patches, and bug fixes, as well as improvement and support for newer hardware that you have integrated into your system. Windows, on the other hand, has an inconsistent release cycle. Sometimes it can take years for a reliable release with some of the releases being poor and full of bugs, really not even worth upgrading to.

Total Control

Using Windows can sometimes feel as though you are on a runaway train. You have applications and processes opening that you have very little understanding of. Sometimes you many not even know what a program is, or what it is doing to your computer. This can be not only confusing, but it can also take up precious memory which should be allocated to the programs you want and need. With Linux, you have greater control over what applications are running and updating, as well as when they do so. You will need to give permission before a program opens so you always know exactly what is occurring on your computer.

You also have full control over the GUI that is operating on your system. If you wanted to change the type of GUI you are using with Windows, you would be unable to do so as you only have one default GUI. Linux offers an extensive variety of GUIs, which are (ironically) called Window Managers. You can select a GUI that you feel works best for the way you use your system. There are dozens of options, from beautiful graphic-heavy GUIs to fast, streamlined options.

Bundles

Windows generally avoids bundling applications with the operating system other than a simple text editor, an image-editing application, and a few others. Many of the applications that are worthwhile require external downloading and installation and often come with a high price tag. Linux bundles many different applications with the distributions. These range from some of the more well-known programs like the Office Suite and photo-editing software, to some open source applications that might be new to you. The advantage is that these applications will come with your distribution free of charge. They improve your computer experience with no extra fees involved. Some of these open source programs are available to download and use on a Windows system, but this takes download and installation time, whereas with Linux they are already available by default. These bundles can be massive, with thousands of applications, some boasting over 20,000 of them.

For those applications that you do need to download onto your system, you can do this through the included app store. With Ubuntu, the built-in app store has thousands of applications which can be easily downloaded with a single click.

Browsing Benefits

Most Linux distributions come bundled with Mozilla Firefox, which most of you will be familiar with. Firefox is a powerful browser with a number of built-in features, such as ad-blocking, pop-up restriction, and a number of other advantages over the standard browser packaged with Windows. Linux also makes browsing simpler and faster due to Linux's improved networking capabilities that save bandwidth and ensure a stable internet connection.

No Automatic Updates

Automatic updates are often touted as a benefit of Windows, but this process can be not only annoying, but also harmful to the ways in which you are using your system. Most people probably have no idea what files are actually being updated. With Linux, you have the option to click and apply the update rather than this happening without your consent. You are welcome to set up your own automatic updates if you wish, but you do not have to just accept them. With Linux, you are given total control over when, how, and what your computer will be updating.

3-D Desktop

Linux allows users to take advantage of an advanced 3-D desktop with Compiz, allowing you to switch and view multiple desktops simultaneously. This feature was considered quite advanced when it was created, miles ahead of Windows. Even now, Compiz is one of the most streamlined 3-D desktops and takes up little memory on the graphics cards.

Chapter 6: Disk Storage Management

In this chapter we will look at how to deal with storage devices and filesystems, this includes naming the devices, partition types and schemes, as well as mounting and unmounting partitions.

Naming the Devices

Everything in Linux is a file, a directory is a file and a device is a file too. Every drive on the system is represented as a block device inside the /dev folder. When the system starts up, the "udev" service is run, which detects all devices in /dev and then mounts them accordingly.

Inside /dev, IDE drives have the names "hda", "hdb" all the way up to "hdp". Other device types such as SCSI, USB, SATA, and PATA are represented as "sda", "sdb" up to "sdp". Drives such as CD or DVD drives receive labels like "cdrom" or "dvd" whereas it is common that SD cards are labeled with "mmcblk".

Each drive must have at least one partition if it is to run on the system. A drive can have up to 16 partitions, each with its own filesystem. Within each device, partitions are then labeled "sda1", "sda2" up to "sda16" for the device /dev/sda. Linux has a limit of sixteen drives with sixteen partitions each.

Primary, Extended, and Logical Partitions

Each drive can have up to four primary partitions, or three primary partitions and one extended partition. Furthermore, an extended partition can contain up to sixteen logical partitions. If a system contains only four primary partitions, they are numbered sda1 through sda4 as follows:

```
/dev/sda1

/dev/sda2

/dev/sda3

/dev/sda4
```

If a system contains three primary partitions and one extended partition, which contains logical partitions, primary partition sda4 falls away and is replaced with logical partitions sda5, sda6, sda7 etc:

```
/dev/sda1
/dev/sda2
/dev/sda3
/dev/sda5
/dev/sda6
/dev/sda7
```

The first logical partition is always numbered as sda5. So even if there are less than three primary partitions, they are numbered as follows:

/dev/sda1

/dev/sda5

/dev/sda6

In order to see the partition structure, the command *lsblk* from the "util-linux" package is quite helpful. *lsblk* abbreviates "list block devices". *lsblk* can output all the block devices that are in use (see first image below) as well as all the unused devices (see second image below).

The six columns represent the following information:

- *NAME - the name of the device.*

- *MAJ:MIN - the major and the minor number of the device.*

- *RM - 0 if the device is fixed, and 1 if the device can be removed.*

- *SIZE - the size of the device in a human-readable format.*

- *TYPE - the type of device. "Loop" represents a loop device, "disk" a hard disk, "part" refers to a partition of a disk, "lvm" is a partition run by a Logical Volume Manager (LVM), and "rom" refers to a CD/DVD rom.*

- *MOUNTPOINT - lists the directory the device is mounted on*

To list the mounted filesystems, use either the *mount* command or the *findmnt* command. Both commands are part of the "mount" package. Invoked without further options, *findmnt* prints all the mounted filesystems. This list can be quite long. In order to only select the ext4 filesystems the option *-t ext4* (short for --type ext4) is can be used.

The four output columns contain the following information:

- *TARGET - the mount point, which is the directory the device is mounted on in the system.*

- *SOURCE - the device name.*

- *FSTYPE - the filesystem type.*

- *OPTIONS - the options which were used to mount the device.*

udev and df

"udev" is the abbreviation for "userspace /dev" and is a device manager for the Linux kernel. Once "udev" runs, the drives it found are shown in the directory /dev/disk. This contains a number of subdirectories with symbolic links as listed below. Note that the number of subdirectories is specific to the Linux release and depends on the version of the Linux kernel. Whenever a disk is recognized by the Linux system, the information is shown here. We can use this information to find which mount points are in use.

/dev/disk/by-id

This shows the partition names that Linux sees and which mount points point to them.

```
# ls -al /dev/disk/by-id
```

/dev/disk/by-path

This shows lower-level hardware definitions and which mount points mount to them.

```
# ls -al /dev/disk/by-path
```

/dev/disk/by-label

This shows which labels are applied to which mount points.

```
# ls -al /dev/disk/by-label
```

/dev/disk/by-uuid

This shows the UUID labels for each mount point.

```
# ls -al /dev/disk/by-uuid
```

/dev/disk/by-partuuid is a component of GUID Partition Tables (GPT) which is a replacement for Master Boot Record (MBR) related disk partitioning.

df

To see which filesystems are mounted, and how many blocks are used and available, invoke the *df* command. *df* is an abbreviation for "disk free". The command offers various options:

- *df -h: List in a human-readable format.*

- *df -k: List in kilobytes.*

- *df -m: List in megabytes.*

- *df: List in default block size. Sometimes this uses 500KB which can be confusing.*

Mounting a Filesystem

Before a filesystem can be used, it must be mounted as part of the directory tree. Most of the time, this is done automatically at startup but can also be done manually.

To demonstrate, we will mount the first partition of the second SCSI disk (/deb/sdb1) as /space. Firstly, in order to mount a filesystem you must be in root. Next, if the directory /space does not exist yet, create it using *mkdir* as follows:

```
# mkdir /space
```

Then run the *mount* command to include this directory:

```
# mount /dev/sdb1 /space
```

Most of the time Linux detects the filesystem type automatically. If this is not the case and the type is not detected automatically, use the *-t* parameter (short for --type) followed by the name of the filesystem type to force it. This step assumes that the relevant filesystem type is installed and recognized by the Linux kernel. To list all the filesystems supported by the Linux kernel, the combination of the commands *cat, awk, sed, ls* and *sort* can be used as follows:

```
$ (cat /proc/filesystems | awk '{print $NF}' | sed '/^$/d'; ls -
1 /lib/modules/$(uname -r)/ -

kernel/fs) | sort -u

9p

adfs
```

```
affs

afs

aufs

autofs

autofs4

bdev

befs

bfs

binfmt_misc

binfmt_misc.ko

btrfs

cachefiles

ceph

...

$
```

The following command extends the commands from above in order to mount the first partition of the second SCSI disk (/deb/sdb1) as /space using an ext3 filesystem [ext3]:

```
# mount -t ext3 /dev/sdb1 /space
```

Unmounting a Filesystem

If the filesystem is busy or in use, it cannot be unmounted. To find out which programs are using the filesystem the *lsof* command from the "lsof" package comes into play. *lsof* abbreviates "list of open files". The image below demonstrates how to use the command, and shows this for the directory /home/user/Music.

This gives a list of programs using the directory. Also if a user is working in that directory, that counts as well, and you will have to change directory with the *cd* command. Next, test if any other programs are using /space by invoking the command *lsof /space*. If any programs are running, stop them and try again. Also, make sure that no terminals are cd'd into /space.

```
$ su

Password:

# lsof /space

...
```

Then type *umount /space*. If you do not get an error message, then /space was successfully unmounted. Alternatively, run the *umount* command with the option *-v* (short for --verbose) in order to see the transaction message. Finally, type *df - k* to see the new partition state.

```
...

# umount /space

# exit

$
```

Automating Mount Points

To automatically mount a mount point during startup of your Linux system, add an entry in the configuration file /etc/fstab. *fstab* abbreviates "file system table". The image below displays the content of the configuration file.

The columns (fields) in the file /etc/fstab are:

• *filesystem - specifies the UUID (UUID=xxxxx), name (/dev/sdb1), or the label of the filesystem (LABEL=home).*

• *mount point - defines the directory where the filesystem will be mounted.*

- *type - a comma-separated list of allowed filesystem types.*

- *options - a comma-separated list of options.*

- *dump - dump information in file with 0 = off, and 1 = on*

- *pass - the order the filesystem is checked starting with 1. 0 means last*

Keep in mind that the single columns are separated by a tabulator, and spaces do not work properly. Tip: to find the UUID for the mount point, look in /dev/disk/by-uuid.

To add a device to mount automatically, extend the file /etc/fstab by simply adding a line. In order to mount the partition /dev/sdb1 as /space with an ext3 filesystem at startup, add this line on older systems:

```
/dev/sdb1 /space ext3 defaults 0 0
```

On contemporary systems that support UUIDs, use the following line. Note to replace the value of "7ca005b2-a7ff-4757-bfdf-81004d4 072ef" by the real UUID of the partition:

```
UUID=7ca005b2-a7ff-4757-bfdf-81004d4072ef /space ext3
defaults 0 0
```

Now /dev/sdb1 will always be mounted as /space at startup. You may wonder what the advantage is of using a UUID. By using a UUID the partition is clearly identified, even if the order of the disks changes later on.

In order to generate a UUID (or to regenerate a new one) use the *uuidgen* command line tool. It offers two options. The first is *-r* (short for --random) which generates a random-based UUID. This method creates a UUID consisting mostly of random bits. This is the default value if not explicitly specified.

```
$ uuidgen -r

4d545248-cf36-4d24-91ab-64a9ed276072

$
```

The second option is -t (short for --time) which generates a time-based UUID. This method creates an UUID based on the system clock plus the system's ethernet hardware address, if present.

```
$ uuidgen -t

4afa1166-bcf1-11e8-9a0a-68f728ff3d63

$
```

The *uuidgen* command writes the newly generated UUID to "stdout". You can copy and paste the new UUID directly into /etc/fstab to have a unique identifier for a partition to be referenced.

Setting up New Partitions

The idea behind *fdisk* and its counterparts, *cfdisk* and *gparted,* is to view the partitions on a disk and to add, remove or edit partitions. Both *cfdisk* and *gparted* are non-standard packages and may require separate installation.

In order to use *fdisk,* as root user type *fdisk* followed by the name of the drive. The next example shows this for the first SCSI disk named /dev/sda:

```
# fdisk /dev/sda
```

This will open a screen as shown below. At the command line prompt press *p* in order to print the partitions:

To get a list of commands available, type *m*, and the following screen will appear. Use *q* to quit *fdisk.*

Creating New Partitions

For the second SCSI disk, start *fdisk* as follows:

```
# fdisk /dev/sdb
```

To create a new partition type "n", first *fdisk* asks us if we would like to create a primary partition or an extended partition. We select *p* for a primary partition. Then *fdisk* asks us what partition number we want. We select *1* for the first partition. Next, it asks for the size. By default *fdisk* fills the entire disk and uses the entire space that is available. We select +*4GB* for a 4GB partition. Then we type *p* to print out the result and we can see the partition /dev/sdb1 has been created.

Now let us add an extended partition. Again, type *n* to create a new partition. This time from the menu we select *e* for an extended partition and hit enter for the default settings, partition 2 and fill all the remaining space. Then type *p* to print out the result and we can see the extended partition /dev/sdb2 has been created.

Now let's create a swap space. Again, type *n* to create a new partition. This time there is no more room for a primary partition, so we can only create a logical partition. We use the default First Sector and select +*1G* for the Last Sector and hit enter for the defaults. Type *p* to see the result and we can see that logical partition /dev/sdb5 has been created. Type *f* to show how much free space is still available on the drive.

Finally, let's create one partition using all the free space. We do the same as with the last partition, except this time we select all the default options. Typing *p* afterward shows us partition /dev/sdb6 has been created.

Now let's change the partition /dev/sdb5 to a swap space. To do this, in *fdisk* type *t* to change the partition type. For partition number we select *5*, and then type *l* to list the available types. The type we want is Linux swap / Solaris. Type *p* to show that the partition's type has changed.

Up to now, nothing has been written to disk. To do this, we need to save and sync disks by typing *w* to write to disk. Now we exit *fdisk* by typing *q* to quit. Type *ls -al /dev/disk/by-id* to see the newly created partitions. As the next step, we will use the newly created partitions to mount filesystems.

Creating New Filesystems

So far we have empty partitions only. These partitions need to be filled with the appropriate filesystems. We will mount the new filesystems as follows:

```
/dev/sdb1 /mnt/root ext2

/dev/sdb5 swap

/dev/sdb6 /mnt/home ext4
```

To do this, first we create the mount points that we need:

```
# mkdir /mnt/root

# mkdir /mnt/home
```

Then to add the filesystems, we issue the following commands:

```
# mkfs /dev/sdb1

# mkfs.ext4 /dev/sdb6
```

Next, we have to set up /dev/sdb5 as a swap partition. *mkswap* creates a swap filesystem, and *swapon* activates the partition as swap space.

```
# mkswap /dev/sdb5

# swapon /dev/sdb5
```

It is a good idea to give each partition its own label. To do this we use *tune2fs* in combination with its option *-L*. The partition /dev/sdb1 is associated with the directory /root, and the partition /dev/sdb6 is associated with the directory /home.

```
# tune2fs -L root /dev/sdb1
```

```
# tune2fs -L home /dev/sdb6
```

Now we can mount the new partitions. Type *df* to see the result.

As the final step let us add entries to the configuration file /etc/fstab in order to be able to auto-mount these filesystems at startup. First make a copy of /etc/fstab as /etc/fstab.bak:

```
# cp /etc/fstab /etc/fstab.bak
```

Then in order to get the block IDs of the new partitions, type *lsblk -f*. The option *-f* (short for --fs) extends the output with additional filesystem information.

Now edit the configuration file /etc/fstab and add the last two lines as shown in the image below.

Then restart the system with your new partitions using *reboot*, and invoke *df* in order to see the newly created partitions.

Chapter 7: Redirecting Commands in Linux

However, this is not the only approach that the commands can use to demonstrate their output. Many command line operating systems like Linux have the capacity to change how the command output is relayed to the user.

This is called *input/output redirection*, and it is used to redirect the result of many commands to files, devices, and sometimes even the inputs of additional commands. In this chapter, you shall get a short introduction to these commands, and how they can be used within Linux to help you get better results.

Standard Input

Linux commands will normally only accept input from the keyboard, also known as the *Standard input*. However, you can redirect this input to a file, which can then be used as the input for a command instead of the keyboard. To do this, the "<" symbol is utilized as follows:

[me@mylinux me]$ sort < file_list.txt

In thisinstance, the sort command is processing the data contained in the file_list.txt file.

Standard Output

The result of the above redirected input will show up on the screen, which is also labeled the *standard output*. However, just as with the standard input, the standard output can be redirected and it is usually redirected to a particular file. This is accomplished using the ">" symbol as follows:

[me@mylinux me]$ ls > name_list.txt

The *ls* command in this example will be successfully executed as usual, however, the output of this command will not appear on the display as is expected, and instead it will be redirected to the file *name_list.txt*.

It is important to note that every time the above command is carried out, it will overwrite the original *name_list.txt*file and create a whole new file. However, if you would like to keep adding to the file rather than overwriting it from the beginning every time, the symbol ">>" should be used as in the example below:

[me@mylinux me]$ ls >> name_list.txt

When this command is run, it will add the new results to the end of the file, making it larger and longer every time it is carried out. If you do attempt to carry out this command and the target file has not been created, Linux will do that for you.

There are situations where the standard input and the standard output need to be redirected. Unlike many other command line programs though, the order in which you write down these commands in Linux does not matter, as long as the characters used to redirect (the "<" and ">") the input and output are in the command line AFTER the options or arguments that they are redirecting then the action will be carried out.

If we were to revert to the standard input command *[me@mylinux me]$ sort < file_list.txt* and change it so that it also has a redirected standard output, the result may resemble something like this:

[me@mylinux me]$ sort < file_list.txt> sorted_file_list.txt

 In this case, the sort command will be executed, and the result shall be saved to the *sorted_file_list.txt* text file.

Using Redirection

Very many different things are possible when redirection. However, one of the most functional uses for redirection is to create what are known as *pipelines*. In the simplest sense, pipelines are astring of commands, where the standard output of one command is linked to the standard input of another. For instance, one of the simplest ones to memorize and use is:

[me@mylinux me]$ ls –l | less

In thisinstance, the product of the *ls* command turns into the input for the *less* command. By doing this, you can create a scrolling output for almost any command you choose. This may not be a very useful technique, but it is fun to watch when it is tried with different commands.

Stringing different commands together in this way can produce some very fascinating results. Listed below are a couple of the more interesting things you can do with pipelines:

- *du | sort −nr* – this command will produce a list of all the directories on your system and give you an idea of just how much space they occupy on it. The list that is generated is arranged in descending order with the biggest directories at the beginning of the file.

- *ls −lt | head* –This pipeline lists the 10 most recently created files in the directory that you are in.

- find .−type f −print | wc −l – *This command will show how many files there are in the directory that you are in, and all of the subdirectories it contains.*

Using Pipelines to execute tasks

Of all the different ways pipelines are used, perhaps the most useful way is when they are used to help execute different tasks. Listed below are just two of the tasks that pipelines help make easier to carry out.

1.   Reading tar files: Once you start using more Linux based software, you may begin to notice that many programs come as *gzipped tar* files. These files are basically conventional Unix style tape archive files that are created using *tar*, then compressed using *gzip.*

Gzipped tar files will normally have one of three file extensions, either, ".tar, .gz" or ".tgz". Opening these files can be a tedious process, but by using a pipeline, all you have to do is enter the one line command shown below and you should be able to view the files on any Linux system

tar tzvf name_of_file.tar.gz | less

2.   Sending files to the printer from the command line: Unlike many command line programs, Linux has a program called *lpr* that allows you to print out standard input. This command is normally used with various pipes and filters as shown below:

cat poorly_formatted_report.txt | fmt | pr | lpr

cat unsorted_list_with_dupes.txt | sort | uniq | pr | lpr

The first instancecontains a file that (as you may be able to guess from the name) has been poorly formatted. The pipeline that has been applied to it will not only help format the file but also to print it by doing the following:

-       *cat* is used to read the file. The output of this then becomes the input for *fmt*

-       *fmt* is used to format the file. This formatting is usually limited to creating paragraphs, which then become the input for *pr*

-       *pr* takes the text file that has been read and formatted and created pages out of the content of the file. The output of this is then sent to *lpr*

-       *lpr* takes the now neatly formatted file and sends it to the printer for the final output.

The second example is very similar in that the text file needs to be formatted in some way before it is sent to the printer. In this case, the list that the text file holds needs to be sorted before it can be printed. By examining the command line we can see how this is done:

- 	 *cat* is used to read the text file. As in the first illustration, the outcome of this is converted into the input for *sort*

- 	 *sort* is used to sort the list properly. Once sorted, the file is then sent to *uniq*

- 	 *uniq* is used to delete any recurring information that may appear in the text file. This outcome is then sent to *pr*

- 	 *pr* creates clean, organized pages, and as in the first example, the result is sent to *lpr*

- 	 *lpr* sends the now sorted, paginated text file to the printer for the final output.

Filters

You may notice in the two examples above that there are a couple of new commands that you may not be familiar with, such as *uniq, fmt,* and *pr.* These are programs that are commonly used within pipelines to perform certain tasks on the standard input and send the result to standard output. Below are a couple of the most frequently used filters, and their purpose:

1. 	 *awk* – This is a very powerful programming language that was created specifically to build filters.

2. 	 *grep* – This program takes each line of data that it receives, analyzes it, and only outputs data that conforms to a particular pattern of characters

3. 	 *fmt* – This program takes unformatted text and outputs a formatted version of the same

4.   *sort* – A program that reads unsorted data and outputs a sorted result

5.   *tr* – This translates different characters, for example, if you would like to change a word from lowercase letters to uppercase letters.

6.   *sed* – This is a more advanced version of *tr* that is able to perform more complex text translations.

Chapter 8: User and Group Management

In this chapter, we will learn about users and groups in Linux and how to manage them and administer password policies for these users. By the end of this chapter, you will be well versed with the role of users and groups on a Linux system and how they are interpreted by the operating system. You will learn to create, modify, lock and delete user and group accounts, which have been created locally. You will also learn how to manually lock accounts by enforcing a password-aging policy in the shadow password file.

Users and Groups

In this section, we will understand what users and groups are and what is their association with the operating system.

Who is a user?

Every process or a running program on the operating system runs as a user. The ownership of every file lies with a user in the system. A user restricts access to a file or a directory. Hence, if a process is running as a user, that user will determine the files and directories the process will have access to.

You can know about the currently logged-in user using the *id* command. If you pass another user as an argument to the id command, you can retrieve basic information of that other user as well.

If you want to know the user associated with a file or a directory, you can use the *ls -l* command and the third column in the output shows the username.

You can also view information related to a process by using the *ps* command. The default output to this command will show processes running only in the current shell. If you use the *ps a* option in the command, you will get to see all the process across the terminal. If you wish to know the user associated with a command, you can pass the *u* option with the ps command and the first column of the output will show the user.

The usernames are mapped to numbers using a database in the system. There is a flat file stored at /etc/passwd, which stored the information of all users. There are seven fields for every user in this file.

username: password:UID:GID:GECOS:/home/dir:shell

username:

Username is simply the pointing of a user ID UID to a name so that humans can retain it better.

password:

This field is where passwords of users used to be saved in the past, but now they are stored in a different file located at /etc/shadow

UID:

It is a user ID, which is numeric and used to identify a user by the system at the most fundamental level

GID:

This is the primary group number of a user. We will discuss groups in a while

GECOS:

This is a field using arbitrary text, which usually is the full name of the user

/home/dir:

This is the location of the home directory of the user where the user has their personal data and other configuration files

shell:

This is the program that runs after the user logs in. For a regular user, this will mostly be the program that gives the user the command line prompt

What is a group?

Just like users, there are names and group ID GID numbers associated with a group. Local group information can be found at /etc/group

There are two types of groups. Primary and supplementary. Let's understand the features of each one by one.

Primary Group:

• There is exactly one primary group for every user

- The primary group of local users is defined by the fourth field in the /etc/passwd file where the group number GID is listed

- New files created by the user are owned by the primary group

- The primary group of a user by default has the same name as that of the user. This is a User Private Group (UPG) and the user is the only member of this group

Supplementary Group:

- A user can be a member of zero or more supplementary groups

- The primary group of local users is defined by the last field in the /etc/group file. For local groups, the membership of the user is identified by a comma separated list of user, which is located in the last field of the group's entry in /etc/group

- groupname: password: GID:list, of, users, in, this, group

- The concept of supplementary groups is in place so that users can be part of more group and in turn have to resources and services that belong to other groups in the system

Getting Superuser Access

In this section, we will learn about what the root user is and how you can be the root or superuser and gain full access over the system.

The root user

There is one user in every operating system that is known as the super user and has all access and rights on that system. In a Windows based operating system, you may have heard about the superuser known as the *administrator*. In Linux based operating systems, this superuser is known as the *root* user. The root user has the power to override any normal privileges on the file system and is generally used to administer and manage the system. If you want to perform tasks such as installing new software or removing an existing software, and other tasks such as manage files and directories in the system, a user will have to escalate privileges to the root user.

Most devices on an operating system can be controlled only by the root user, but there are a few exceptions. A normal user gets to control removable devices such as a USB drive. A non-root user can, therefore, manage and remove files on a removable device but if you want to make modifications to a fixed hard drive, that would only be possible for a root user.

But as we have heard, with great power comes great responsibility. Given the unlimited powers that the root user has, those powers can be used to damage the system as well. A root user can delete files and directories, remove or modify user accounts, create backdoors in the system, etc. Someone else can gain full control over the system if the root user account gets compromised. Therefore, it is always advisable that you login as a normal user and escalate privileges to the root user only when absolutely required.

It is a practice in Linux to login as a regular user and then use tools to gain certain privileges of the root account.

Using Su to Switch Users

You can switch to a different user account in Linux using the *su* command. If you do not pass a username as an argument to the su command, it is implied that you want to switch to the root user account. If you are invoking the command as a regular user, you will be prompted to enter the password of the account that you want to switch to. However, if you invoke the command as a root user, you will not need to enter the password of the account that you are switching to.

su - <username>

[student@desktop ~]$ su -

Passord: rootpassword

[root@desktop ~]#

If you use the command su username, it will start a session in a non-login shell. But if you use the command as su - username, there will be a login shell initiated for the user. This means that using su - username sets up a new and clean login for the new user whereas just using su username will retain all the current settings of the current shell. Mostly, to get the new user's default settings, administrators usually use the su - command.

sudo and the root

There is a very strict model implemented in linux operating systems for users. The root user has the power to do everything while the other users can do nothing that is related to the system. The common solution, which was followed in the past was to allow the normal user to become the root user using the su command for a temporary period until the required task was completed. This, however, has the disadvantage that a regular user literally would become the root user and gain all the powers of the root user. They could then make critical changes to the system like restarting the system and even delete an entire directory like /etc. Also, gaining access to become the root user would involve another issue that every user switching to the root user would need to know the password of the root user, which is not a very good idea.

This is where the *sudo* command comes into the picture. The sudo command lets a regular user run command as if they are the root user, or another user, as per the settings defined in the /etc/sudoers file. While other tools like su would require you to know the password of the root user, the sudo command requires you to know only your own password for authentication, and not the password of the account that you are trying to gain access to. By doing this, it allows the administrator of the system to allow a certain list of privileges to regular users such that they perform system administration tasks, without actually needing to know the root password.

Lets us see an example where the student user through sudo has been granted access to run the *usermod* command. With this access, the student user can now modify any other user account and lock that account

[student@desktop ~]$ sudo usermod -L username

[sudo] password for student: studentpassword

Another benefit of using the sudo access is that all commands that any user runs using sudo are logged to */var/log/secure*.

Chapter 9: Commands and Functions for the Beginner

Here we present two guides for the Linux newbie. The first will be a handy cheat sheet so to speak. If you have to memorize anything for the desktop or server, this is the way to go. The second list is more comprehensive, but again, it is not the end of the Commands needed to truly advance to novice levels with Linux.

LIST OF TOP 35 COMMANDS FOR BEGINNERS- IF YOU HAVE TO MEMORIZE THEM

1. apt-get Search for software packages and install
2. bzip2   Compress/decompress a file
3. cd   Change Directory
4. chmod   Change access permissions for a file
5. cp   Copy one or more files or directories location
6. date   Display or set the date & time
7. df   Display free and used disk space
8. emacs   Text editor
9. exit   Exit shell
10. find   Search for files that meet a certain pattern
11. hostname Print or change system name
12. install Copy files, set/change attributes

13. locate   Search and find files

14. ls   List information about directory contents

15. man   Display help information for a certain command

16. mkdir   Create new folder/directory

17. mv   Move or rename directories and files

18. nano   Text editor with shortcuts to menus

19. open   Open a file in original application

20. ps   Display of current process status

21. pwd   Display/Print working directory

22. quota   Display disk use, limits

23. reboot Reboot system

24. rm   Remove, delete directories or files

25. rmdir   Remove, delete, empty directories or folders

26. shutdown Shutdown or restart

27. sftp   Secure File Transfer Program

28. sudo   Execute command as certain user with all permissions

29. tar   Store, list or extract files from a tarfile or tarball/archive

Chapter 10: Using Linux Text Editors

Even though you are capable of using a desktop that has a functional graphic interface, you will find the desire to interact with the Linux environment by editing and creating files using editors that belong outside the GUI. Learning how to use text editors will allow you to make your own shell scripts and communicate with the programs that you want to run in your operating system. At the same time, you will also be able to fix possible problems in your configuration files, especially when the X Window System fails to load.

In this chapter, you will learn how to use GUI and text mode editors, which will both allow you to configure and create text files.

How to Use GUI Text Editors

The GUI desktops KDE and GNOME comes with built-in text editors that have their own graphical user interfaces. You can load these editors from the main menu. For example, if you want to open the GUI text editor for GNOME, navigate to Applications->Text Editor and then select the file gedit. Once the editor loads, you can select the Open option found on the toolbar and then pull up a file that you want to edit or change directories that contain the file that you want in the dialog box labeled Open File.

GNOME's text editor is also capable of loading multiple files at a time and even switch in between windows to work with them. A typical editing session will look like this:

Image from: Linux All-in-One for Dummies

Looking at this image, you will notice that there are two files loaded in the editor – one appears to be a new file, and the other is named motd. You can find the names of the files that are being edited in the tabs, which you can also click to switch windows.

If you open a file that is only available to be read, you will see a text that displays "Read Only" added to the filename displayed in the window title. If you have access to superuser privileges, you can of course change the ownership of the file in order for you to make edits.

If you have a KDE desktop, you can pull up the KWrite text editor by navigating to Applications -> Accessories -> Text Editor.

Just like in the GNOME text editor, you can click on the Open icon or navigate to File -> Open in order to load the file that you want to edit. This is how the KWrite editor looks like:

Image from: Linux All-in-One for Dummies

Using ed and vi as Text Editors

As you may have noticed, text editors that have GUIs allow you to edit files using your mouse and keyboard similar to how you would type a document in a word processor. However, text mode editors are more complex than that – you only have your keyboard as you input device and you will have to type in commands in order to perform tasks such as copying, pasting, or cutting texts.

Text editors that come native with Linux are called ed and vi.

ed

This line oriented editor is going to be extremely useful when you loaded a minimal version of the OS and you do not have the support that you need yet for a full-screen editor yet. You may encounter this situation when you load up Linux from a boot disk.

Using ed allows you to work in these modes:

• Command mode – this is the default mode, in which everything that you type is being interpreted by Linux as a command. In this mode, ed has a rather simple set of commands, wherein each command is made up of one or multiple characters.

• Text input mode – this mode is for typing longer texts. You can enter this mode when you enter the commands a (meaning append), c (meaning change), or i (meaning insert). When you are done entering several lines of text, you can leave this mode by putting only a period on an empty line.

To practice using ed as an editor, perform the following commands:

This will copy the file /etc/fstab in your home directory. To start editing this file, key in this command;

The editor will then respond to display this output:

From this example, the −p option allowed you to set the colon (the symbol :) as your prompt and also opened the fstab file copy that you have in your home directory. Each time the ed editor pulls up a file for editing, it displays the number of charaters that are within the editable file and then displays the colon prompt that signals you can enter your commands through the editor.

Tip: when you want to edit using ed, see to it that you have that you have turned on the prompt using the −p option. This will help you distinguish that you are in the text input mode and not in the command mode.

Once ed has opened up a file that you want to edit, you will immediately be in the last line of the file. To see what the current line number is, or the line where the command that you are going to input is going to be placed, you can use the .= command, which will appear like this:

From this result, you know now that the file fstab contains 9 lines. Now, if you want to see all the lines that are contained in the file, you can use the following command:

```
1,$p
```

This will return with an output that appears like this:

If you want to go to a line number that you want to edit (line 2, for example), simply type in the line number on the prompt. The editor will then respond by displaying that particular line:

If, for example, you want to delete a line that contains the word cdrom, all you need to do is to search for that particular string. You can do this by typing the / sign, then the string that you need to find:

This will return with the line that contains the line that you want to edit, which becomes the current line. To delete it, simply enter d on the prompt.

To replace a specific string with a different one, the s command will be handy to use. For example, if you want to replace the string "cdrom" with "cd", enter this command:

To input a line in front of the line that you are currently editing, use the following command:

From this point, you can enter as many lines that you want. If you are done typing, enter the period sign on an empty line to indicate that you are ending the text input mode. After doing so, you will see that ed switches back to the command mode.

If you want to save the changes that you have made to the file, enter the w command on the prompt. If you want to save the changes and exit the editor, key in wq on the prompt to perform both actions. The output will appear like this:

The editor will then save all changes that you have performed and then display the number of characters that were saved. Afterwards, Linux will exit the editor. However, if you want to exit without saving any changes that you have made to the file, key in the q command to exit without writing to the file.

Of course, there are different other commands that you can use in ed. Here is a summary of the most common commands used in the ed editor:

Image from: Linux All-in-One for Dummies

vi

The editor vi is definitely easier to use compared to ed, although it is still considered as a command line editor. The vi allows you to use a text editor in a full screen mode, which means that you can view multiple lines at the same time. It also helps to know that most of the Unix systems (this includes Linux) come with this text editor; which means that once you understand how this editor works, you will be able to modify text files in any system that is based in Unix.

Note: When you edit a text file using vi, the editor reads it into a buffer memory. This means that you can change the file in the buffer. At the same time, this editor also makes use of temporary files during an edit session, which means that no changes are made in the original file unless you save any changes that you made.

To start editing with vi, key in vi followed by the filename:

This will allow vi to load the file, then display the first lines of the text file in to the screen. The cursor will also be positioned on the first line:

Image from: Linux All-in-One for Dummies

The last line that you see in this example shows the pathname, along with the number of lines and characters in the file. You will also notice that the file is read-only. This means that you are viewing the file as a normal user. You may have also noticed that since the number of lines does not occupy the rest of your screen, the unused lines are marked with the tilde (~) sign. The current line is marked by a black rectangle on top of the character that is being edited.

The vi editor allows you to enter the following modes:

•   Visual command – this is the default mode, wherein everything that you key in is considered by Linux as a command to be applied to the current line. All vi commands are the same as ed commands.

•   Colon command – this mode is set for writing or reading files, setting up options for vi, and exiting vi. As the name implies, all commands in this mode start with the colon. When you key in the colon symbol, the editor moves the cursor to the last line and then prompts you to enter the command. The editor will apply the command once you hit the Enter key.

•   Text input – this is the mode that you need to use when you want to enter text into the file. You are able to enter this mode when you use the following commands:

Once you are done typing in your text, press Esc to exit this mode and return to visual command.

Tip: It may be a bit difficult to tell what command mode you are in when you are using the vi editor. There may be circumstances that you have typed a long line of text only to realize that you are not in the text input mode, which can be a little frustrating. If you want to see to it that you are in command mode, press Esc a couple of times.

It is also helpful to know that you can make use of the arrow keys and some keyboard to move the cursor and the screen around. Try these commands out:

Image from: Linux All-in-One for Dummies

You can also jump to a specific line using the colon command. For example, if you want to switch immediately to line 6, just type 6 after the colon and then hit Enter:

Keep in mind that when you enter the colon symbol, the vi editor will display it at the last line of the screen. After doing so, vi will consider any text that you enter as a command.

To search for a particular string, key in the / symbol and then hit Enter. The / symbol will appear at the last line, which prompts you to enter the string that you want to search for. Once it is found, vi will position the cursor at the beginning of the matching entry in a line of the text. For example, if you want to search for the string "cdrom" in the /etc/fstab file, key in:

If you wish to delete the line where the cursor is placed, type the command dd. The editor will then delete that line and then change into the next line as the current line.

If you wish to enter text at the cursor, type the command i. The editor will change its mode to become text input, which will then allow you to type in your desired text. Once you are done, hit Esc. The vi editor will revert to visual command afterwards.

Once you are done modifying the file, you can save changes that you have made by entering the :w command. To save the file and exit the editor, enter the :wq command. Alternatively, you can also perform save and exit at the same time by holding down the Shift key and then hitting Z twice.

To exit the editor without saving, enter the :q! command.

Here are other commands that are commonly used by the vi editor:

Image from: Linux All-in-One for Dummies

Chapter 11: Coding with Linux

The basics of the coding language are pretty similar throughout: you have a command line, you have executed a command line, and you have the idea of utilizing those command lines in order to change or interface with the operating system.

Have I already lost you? Let's break it down.

A command line is a string of letters, numbers, and characters typed into a terminal window. Whenever you are watching television shows that have the computer whiz pulling up a black screen to type little green letters into, that black box is the terminal window. The green letters and lines? That's a command line.

Those command lines, when executed, tell the operating system to do different things. So, you type in a specific line, execute it, and the computer does what you have told it to do in that line.

Sounds a bit like parenting, right?

The command line interface, and how it interacts with the desktop environment and user interface, is one of the many strengths of the Linux-based operating systems. There are versions of every desktop environment that you can download onto your technological device that allow you to interact with the Linux system based solely on those terminal windows. When you open up the main desktop environment of a computer, there's usually a pretty background picture and a button for the start menu. Maybe there are some folders you can click on or some applications you can open. With a command line interface, that pretty little background image becomes a massive terminal window—your interface with the computer by entering command lines.

Want to open the main menu? There's a command line you execute.

Want to download an application? There's a command line you execute.

Obviously, this type of interface is for experts, but you get the picture. Linux is capable of it all, and no other operating system has that type of interface available for free.

Yes, free.

The first thing you need when interacting with a terminal window to program on a Linux system is to get to the shell. The shell is a particular program that helps turn the text you type in that terminal window into executable command lines. Think of it this way: you are baking a cake, and you have put all the ingredients together. You've mixed everything up, you pour it into the baking tin, and now you're ready for your cake to appear.

What do you do next?

You put it in the oven to bake, of course.

The shell is that oven: without it, the ingredients you mixed together (or the text you typed in the terminal window) don't do anything.

The shell brings the heat.

There are many different shells that are available for Linux, but the most popular one is Bash (also known as the "Bourne-Again" shell). Start with this one and see what you think.

Now, listen up: obviously, since you are a beginner, you are not starting out with a command line interface desktop environment. You've chosen the one with the pretty background and the easily-clickable things. Don't worry, everyone loves them. What you'll need, however, to access the terminal window to practice your coding is a terminal emulator. All of the distributions of Linux come with their own emulators, so unless you want to download a different one for some reason, the legwork has already been done for you.

So, what was the point of mentioning it?

Well, it's just good to know.

So, coding with Linux begins with very basic commands you can execute and watch. When you first open a terminal emulator, you are automatically logged into your computer's home directory as a user. This means you should see some sort of username followed by a hostname. Keep in mind that "swapnil" will be the default username we use, but it will be your own username that's assigned to your Linux operating system that you'll need to use for these commands.

Commit these two things to memory: *$* means you are logged in as a regular user, and *#* means you are logged in as a root. What is a root? Well, it's the user who has access to all the files and commands a Linux system has at its disposal. Think of the "root" as the "master."

So, open up your first terminal window and type this:

[swapnil@swaparch ~]$ ls

This will bring up a list of all the directories and files currently inside your Linux operating system.

Cool, huh?

Now, there's the idea of moving around. If you want to change any single directory, use a *cd* command, and use the forward slash (/) to enter the contents of those directories. For example, if you want to change the "Downloads" directory, you'll want to run a cd command line and then give it a path.

To access the "Downloads" directory, enter this: *Documents/ Downloads/*

Then, enter these two lines:

[swapnil@swaparch ~]$ cd /home/swapnil/Downloads/

[swapnil@swaparch Downloads]$

The first line you typed in got you into the "Downloads" directory. The second line enabled you, as a main user (as denoted by the "$" sign), to implement a change to the "Downloads" directory (as denoted by the "cd"). The third line, with the word "Downloads" inside the brackets, makes it possible for you to navigate within that directory. "Downloads" inside the brackets means you are now accessing the innards of that directory.

The great thing about that third line is you can now use it to navigate within the subcategories of that directory. You don't have to go through the whole process just to get there. So, if you want to access the "Test" sub-category buried within the "Downloads" directory, all you have to do is type this:

[swapnil@swaparch Downloads]$ cd Test

Then, if you want to get out of the current directory and simply go back home, type this:

cd

Yep, just "cd."

Another fun thing is to access is hidden files within certain directories. In order to access these hidden corridors, you have to execute a "-a" option within the "ls" command. So, using the "Test" sub-category of the "Downloads" directory, type this:

[swapnil@swaparch ~]$ ls -a /home/swapnil/Downloads/Test/

This will pull up a list of hidden files and directories that you can slowly navigate your way through as you play around with the basics!

And don't worry—if you muck up something that permanently alters your Linux operating system, simply put in your USB thumb drive or the live CD you burned that houses the operating system, reboot your computer, and reinstall Linux onto your technological device.

Another basic to know is how to create directories. The basic command signal within the command line for creating a new directory is "mkdir." So, the basic formula for creating a new directory looks like this:

mkdir   /path-of-the-parent-directory/name-of-the-new-directory

"Path of the parent directory" means the main directory you want to put the new one in. Is it part of "Downloads"? Is it part of "Home"?

"Name of the new directory" is just what you want to call it. It can be as serious as "Things I Need To Remember" or as silly as "JumpingBeanJellyDonut." Get creative! This is the fun part of programming with Linux.

For example, if you want to create a directory entitled "distros" inside of the "Downloads" directory, the command line you'll run looks like this:

```
[swapnil@swaparch ~]$ mkdir
/home/swapnil/Downloads/distros
```

That's enough to get you started for now. Become comfortable with these programming basics before you dedicate yourself to going any further. If you are feeling overwhelmed, take a long, slow breath. It's overwhelming at first because it's essentially working with another language entirely, but the same basic formulas stay in place. Just like a sentence and grammatical structure stay the same in a language no matter the dialect, so does the order in which you have to enter information in order to access a category or its sub.

More Linux commands

The next command you need to learn about is Print Working Directory, or pwd. Most of the commands in Linux are abbreviations of their full terms or the words that describe what they do, which makes it so much easier to remember what they are! This command does exactly that—it tells you what the present working directory is, the one you are in at the time you call the command.

pwd

/home/Cleopatra

Lots of terminal commands will only work properly if you are in the right place and, as you'll be moving from one place to another frequently, it can easily become difficult to forget where you are.

The pwd command will keep you on track, so use it as often as you need to.

The current location

Ok, so knowing where you are is one thing, but what about what is in your current location?

ls

bin Documents public_html

While pwd runs alone without any arguments, ls is quite a bit more powerful. However, we can do some more with this so look at this:

ls [options] [location]

Chapter 12: Programming in Linux using Python

Well, this is true. C++ is a lot denser of a language than Python, which is made for rapid prototyping and quick, messy scripting. In no way is C++ meant for either of these! However, that means that C++ and Python have a lot of differences that make it a little bit better to learn C++ first, just to be a better programmer.

First off, when you learn C++ first, you're learning to be mindful of your resource usage. Python takes care of a lot for you. For example, you don't have to worry about the value of a variable when passing to a function, and you don't really have to worry that a variable is just going to be a copy of a variable, and you especially don't have to worry about freeing up memory that you're using. When you learn C++ first, you learn to be mindful of these things from the get-go, because there are ways to be mindful of them in Python as well simply by following good practices and not being immensely wasteful in the very essence of your code.

Second off, when you learn C++ first, you're learning to be more mindful of *what you're making*. You have to explicitly type every function and variable, instead of just letting it be implied. This also forces you to bear it in mind as you play around with different variables and start to become a better programmer. When you're starting out, you'll have to pay attention to the fact that variable *c* is an int while variable *d* is a string. You don't have to worry about this as much in Python, but it's good practice to keep things like value types in your head all the time as you're working on a language.

So with all of this said, there are a *lot* of advantages to learning Python, too. First off, it's one of the most commonly learned and used programming languages in the world today. This means that there is a huge amount of documentation available to you as a novice Python programmer - and a lot of people who have asked the same questions that you likely will have, which means that there are people who have already given answers out there, too.

More than that, Python is just a very clean and effective language. Many people who have worked with Python have grown to love it, myself included. When you know what you're doing with programming, working with Python is a pretty fun and fast experience. Many of the things that bog you down in other languages simply fail to exist or have a measurable impact in Python.

If you're running Linux, then you should already have Python, which simplifies the whole setup process quite a bit. You can test this out by opening up the Terminal and then typing *python* and pressing enter. If it launches Python, then you're all set. If not, you'll need to go to Python.org and get it, but this really shouldn't be an issue on Linux distributions.

If it launches as anything other than Python 2.7.12, then you need to downgrade. There's no reason for it to launch as Python 3 because the standard among Linux distributions is Python 2.7 as of the time of writing, but it's still a case of better safe than sorry. Python 2 and Python 3 are different beasts, and the majority of the code that you can work with in Python will be written in Python 2 just because it's been out for so much longer. Python 3 is still relatively bleeding edge software, even now. Python 2 and Python 3 aren't hugely different, but there are small differences that make a big impact in your learning. If you ever need to learn Python 3, then the transition will be extremely easy to the point of being pretty much a non-factor, so don't worry about that. We're learning Python 2 simply because there's a lot more software available for it, plus it should be the version already bundled with your Linux installation.

You launch Python files from the command line simply by typing *python filename.py*, where filename.py is, of course, the Python file in question. All Python files end in .py.

Your First Program

Python is much simpler than C++. There is no empty shell that we need to work with, you simply need to *start*. Create a new file and save it under whatever name you'd like to so that you get syntax highlighting. Afterward, you need to just type the following in it:

print "hello world\n"

Then save it and run it from the Terminal. It should print the following:

hello world

If it did, then congrats! Your first Python script has been written!

Variables and Values

Variables and values are far easier in Python. The types are pretty much the same, except that there isn't much differentiation between chars and strings in Python. Most of the time, you'll just be using strings. Create variables by simply naming them then assigning a value. Create a new file named whatever you like, then type the following:

bananas = 3

favoriteFruit = "bananas"

print "My favorite fruit is %s, and I have %d!" % (favoriteFruit, bananas)

Save it and then run it from Terminal. It should print:

My favorite fruit is bananas, and I have 3!

If so, then great. Everything is working just fine. What we just did there was called printing a formatted string. That's actually a C skill and not a C++ skill. However, it's the easiest way to print things in Python, so become familiar. The way it works should be fairly obvious given context. Here are the different formatting types you will likely use:

%s-strings

%d-integers

%f-floating points (use %#f for precision, e.g. %2f for two decimals)

%r-raw data, no extra formatting, mainly for debugging

Data Sets

Every data set in Python is just a list. Lists are dynamic arrays, much like vectors and sets. Let's refer back to the studentGrades example. You can create an empty list, like so:

studentOneGrades = []

Or you can populate it with data from the start:

studentOneGrades = [99, 93, 97] # and so on...

In Python lists, you can also use more than one data type! This means you can have things like integers, strings, and even custom-made objects in the same list. For right now, stick to just having one, though - it keeps things neat.

You can add an item to a list using the append method:

studentOneGrades.append(95) # What a good grade!

Then you can remove an item by using the del keyword and referring to its index, which works the same exact way as C++ arrays do:

del studentOneGrades[3]

If you remove something in the middle of a list, every list element in front of it moves back one index spot.

Comparison and Conditionals

These work almost exactly the same as they do in C++. The only difference is the syntax of if, else if, and else statements. Here is a single statement involving all so that you can get a feel for the syntax:

if age >= 18:

print "You are an adult!"

elif age < 18 and age >= 13:

print "You are a teenager!"

else:

print "You are a child!"

Note that *not*, *and*, and *or* are spelled out in Python.

Also note the indentation and lack of braces. Whitespace DOES matter

in Python.

Loops

Python loops are actually incredibly straightforward. While loops function almost identically to their C++ counterpart, just with Pythonic syntax. Here is counting from 1 to 10 using a while loop:

i = 1

```
while i <= 10:

print i


I += 1
```

```
# note that increments by one and decrements by one don't exist
in


# PYTHON. YOU MUST USE += OR -=.
```

Meanwhile, for loops are relatively different. In C++ and Python alike, they're both used to iterate through something. However, the iterative purpose in Python is far clearer. In order to use a for loop in Python, you have to have a list for it to iterate through. The syntax for a Python for loop is like so:

for *iterator* in *list*:

do something

If you wanted to create a range from 1 to 10, though, you could do that. There's a range method in Python that will return a list of elements between two starting points (or starting from 0 if you don't specify a starting point.) Here is how one would count from 1 to 10 using a for loop:

for i in range(1,10):

print i

The purpose of an iterator variable is to stand in for every object of a list throughout loops regardless of the type and take on the attributes of the current object in the list. This means that if you had a list of words, like so:

sentence = ["I", "like", "cats"]

Then you could print out each word, one line at a time, like so:

for word in sentence:

print word

The iterator variable takes on whatever name you give it and assumes it through the rest of the loop.

Methods

Python methods are rather simple. All that you do is use the *def* keyword, then set up a barebones version. Here's the calculateSquareFootage method set up as a Python method:

def calculateSquareFootage(l, w):

return l * w

Then here is a call to that method:

print calculateSquareFootage(4,5)

would print 20

That sums up the largest parts of Python scripting. There's a lot more to it, but these are the largest components that you need to know as a new programmer.

Chapter 13: Advanced Shell Programming

In the first part of this book you were introduced to shell programming and most of its basics were explored. Now we are going to explore the advanced features of shell programming.

Functions in Shell

Shell functions have the following syntax:

function_name ( ) command

They are usually laid out as follows:

function_name() {

    Commands
}

There are different exit statuses for functions in a shell. By default they will return an exit status of zero (0). The programmer should specify the exit status needed. It is also possible to define variables locally within a shell function.

 Consider the shell program shown below:

#!/bin/sh

function_increment() {   # we start by defining the increment so as to use it

```
echo $(($1 + $2))

# this will echo the result after addition of the first and the
second parameters
}

# checking for the availability of all the command line arguments

if [ "$1" "" ] || [ "$2" = "" ] || [ "$3" = "" ]

then

echo USAGE:

echo "   counter initialvalue incrementvalue finalvalue"

else

c=$1                    # renaming variables having clearer names

value=$2

final=$3

while [ $c -lt $final ]    # if the c is less than final, then loop

do

echo $c

c=$(function_increment $c $value)  2# Calling for increment
with c and value as the parameters

done                    # the c will be incremented by value
```

fi

Note how we have begun by defining our function. We have then added together the first and second parameters being passed into the function. The use of the "*echo*" command will print the result to the standard output. For referencing purposes we use command substitution. This is the line "c=$(function_increment $c $value)".

The parameters "*c*" and "value" will be passed into the line where we specified the first and second argument being passed into the function, which is the line "echo $(($1 + $2))". These will then be added together and the result will be printed on the standard output.

Scope of variables

Consider the shell program shown below:

```
#!/bin/sh
function_increment() {

    local v=5

    echo "The value is $v within the function\\n"

    echo "\\b\$1 is $1 within the function"

}
v=6
echo "The value is $v before the function"
```

echo "\\$1 is $1 before the function"

echo

echo -e $(function_increment $v)

echo "The value is $v after the function"

echo "\\$1 is $1 after the function"

We have begun by assigning a value of 5 to our local variable "*v*" and then specified the desired output. We have then called our function using the following line of code:

echo -e $(function_increment $v)

That is what is called a 'function' in shell programming. The use of the "--*e*" option allows the ability to process the slashes in the correct way. Note the use of "\\N" as a new line character.

 The following output will be observed from the program:

The value is 6 before the function

$1 is 2 before the function

The value is 5 within the function

$1 is 5 within the function

The value is 6 after the function

$1 is 2 after the function

Creating Aliases

In Linux, aliases are used to represent commands. If you need to know all the aliases defined on your machine, run the following command on your terminal:

alias

On the example machine, the above command gave the following result:

The above figure shows the aliases defined on this system. All the above are default aliases. You can create aliases as well.

To create aliases, use the following syntax:

alias name='command'

alias name='command argument1 argument2'

In Linux, the command "*clear*" is used to clear the terminal screen. To use the letter "*s*" to represent the command, that is, create an alias for the command, do the following:

alias s= 'clear"

Run the above command on your terminal. This is demonstrated in the figure shown below:

Since I have used the "*ls*" command to see the files in the directory, I need to clear the terminal. Type the letter "*s*" on the terminal and press the enter key. It will clear the terminal.

The command "*date*" in Linux is used to display the current date. Create an alias for it. Use letter "*d*" as an alias for the same command.

This is demonstrated in the figure shown below:

As shown in the above figure, the letter "*d*" is used as an alias for the "*date*" command. After typing the letter "*d*" on the terminal, press the "*Enter*" key and the current date is displayed.

Aliases are very important in Linux. If you want to save on typing time then create them. The name for an alias should be easy to remember, including the commands that they represent.

You might find the need to delete aliases you have created. This can be achieved as follows:

On this system, I have the following aliases:

Note the presence of the two aliases that were created previously. To delete the alias "d" representing the "*date*" command, run the following command:

unalias d

This is demonstrated in the figure shown below:

As shown in the above figure, after deleting the alias and then trying to use it, the computer states that it is not found.

It is possible to remove more than one alias at once. If you need to remove the aliases "*d*" for "*date*" and "*s*" for "*clear*" the following command should be used:

unalias d s

The above command will delete the two aliases. After running the command you can then run the "*alias*" command to check whether they are still available.

Tilde Expansion in Linux

In most cases Linux users use the tilde (~) symbol to refer to their home directory, while others use the home directory.

To see your home directory file listing run the following command:

ls ~

To view the ".*bashrc*" file located in the home directory, run the following command:

cat ~/.bashrc

ls ~/.bashrc

The first command will open the file on the terminal window. This is demonstrated below:

The second command will show the directory where the file is located. This is shown in the following figure:

If the prefix for the tilde symbol is a plus (+), this will substitute the "*PWD*" command. If it is preceded by a negative sign, or (-), then the variable "OLTDPWD" is substituted if it had been set.

It is worth noting that Linux commands can either be built-in or in an external binary file. To know where a command belongs, we use the "*type*" command.

To find out whether the command "*ls*" is built-in, run the following command:

type –a ls

The above command will give the following output:

To find out whether the "*history*" command is built-in or an external command, run the following command:

type –a history

It is worth noting that some commands in Linux can be both built-in and external.

To demonstrate this, run the following commands:

type –a echo

The above command will give the following output:

Nested "ifs" in Shell

Nested "*if*" means that it is an "*if*" statement inside another "*if*" statement.

It follows the following structure:

if condition

then

if condition

then

. . .

Statement to be executed

else

...

Stamen to be executed

fi

else

...

.....

Statement to be executed

fi

Exit status for commands

After a command executes and terminates either normally or abnormally, it must return an exit status. The exit status is usually an integer value. An exit status of zero (0) means that the command executed successfully. Any other exit status, which can range from 1-255, means that the command failed to execute.

To know the exit status of a previously executed command, use the variable "?", which is a special character in shell.

To determine the exit status, run the following command:

echo $?

This will give the exit status of the previously executed command. In the example system it offers the following result:

The result is a zero (0), meaning that the previously executed command on the system executed successfully.

To demonstrate this practically, begin by running the "*ls*" command on your system. Make sure that it runs successfully. On the example system it gives the following result:

Since it has run successfully, try to check its status using the special shell character.

 Run the following command:

echo $?

The above command should return an exit status of zero (0), since the previous command executed successfully.

 This is demonstrated in the figure shown below:

This time try to run a command that is not recognized and then check the exit status. Run the following command:

ls1

You should be aware that the above command does not exist in Linux. Running it will result in an error.

In the example system it gives the following result:

The output shows that the command has not been found. This means that it does not exist in Linux.

To check its exit status, run the usual command, which is shown below:

echo $?

The above command gives the following output on the example system:

The exit status is not zero (0), meaning that the command did not execute successfully. The returned integer is between 0 and 255, as we initially said. To conclude this, any command whose exit status is not zero did not execute successfully.

Conditional execution in shell

In Linux shell programming it is possible to join two commands, where the execution of the second command will be based on the first.

Logical AND

This takes the following syntax:

1stcommand && 2ndcommand

With this conditional execution, the "2ndcommand" will be executed if and only if the "1stcommand" returned an exit status of zero (0). This means that you should first run the "1stcommand" if the "2ndcommand" runs successfully.

Let's demonstrate this using an example.

In the current directory I have the following file:

Let me try to delete the file named "*file*" and then echo a message afterwards. I run the following command:

rm file && echo "file has been deleted"

The above command will return the following result:

The output clearly shows that the first command ran successfully, followed by the second command. Try to run an incorrect command first to see what happens.

From the list of files in the directory there is no file named "fruits". Try to delete a file with that name and then echo a message afterwards.

Run the following command:

rm fruits && echo "the file has been deleted"

The above command will give the following result:

The command returns an error message. This means that the first command had no exit status of zero since it did not run successfully. If it had run successfully we would have the correct result.

Suppose you want to use the *"grep"* command to search for a particular word or name in a file. You can make use of the logic AND to echo the result. Give the file *"names2"* two names. Search for the name *"caleb"* in the file.

Run the following command:

grep "caleb" names2 && echo "The name was found"

The above command gives the following result:

The above figure shows that the first command exited with an exit status of 0, so the second command was run successfully.

Logic OR

This is a Boolean operator. Programmers can make use of this operator to execute a certain command based on another command.

It takes the following syntax:

1stcommand || 2ndcommand

The command *"2ndcommand"* will be executed if and only if the command *"1stcommand"* executes unsuccessfully, meaning that it returns a non-zero exit status. In other words, you can run only one of the commands. This means that if the first command runs successfully, the second command will be unsuccessful and vice versa.

Consider the following Linux command:

grep "caleb" names2 || echo "The name was not found"

The above command will output the following:

The output shows that the name *"caleb"* was successfully found in the specified file. Note that the second command was not executed. This is because we can only execute one of the commands.

Consider the example command shown below:

grep "john" names2 || echo "The name was not found"

The above command gives the following output:

From the output shown above it is very clear that the second was executed. The first command executed unsuccessfully and this led to the execution of the second command. This is because there is no name *"john"* in the specified file.

This can be demonstrated using another example.

Try to delete a certain file from the current directory. The following command should be used:

rm for.sh || echo "file not deleted"

In the directory there is a file named *"for.sh"*. I then try to delete it. Since the first command succeeds, meaning that the file will be deleted, the second command will not be executed. After running the command I am taken back to the terminal since the operation has been completed.

This is demonstrated in the figure shown below:

What will happen when trying to delete a file that is not present? This is demonstrated using the following example.

Try to delete a file that does not exist in the directory. Run the following command:

rm myfile || echo |file not found"

The above command tries to delete a file that does not exist in the current directory. If the deletion fails, the second part of the command should be executed. In the example system the above command gives the following result:

The first part of the command ran unsuccessfully, meaning that it had a non-zero exit status. This led to the execution of the second part of the command.

It is also possible to combine the two logical operators into one. Consider the command shown below:

grep "caleb" names2 && echo "name found" || echo "not found"

On this system the above command gives the following output:

Note that only the first two commands have been executed. The last command has not been executed. Try to search for a name that is not available in the specified file.

The command below can be used:

grep "john" names2 && echo "name found" || echo "not found"

The above command gives the following output:

It is very clear that the first two parts of the above command have not been executed. The second part of the command will only be executed if the first part of the command returns an exit status of zero (0). This is due to the use of the logical "*AND*" operator.

The last part of the command is executed on its own if and only if the first two parts of the command run unsuccessfully.

Logical Not

This is also a logical operator and it is used for testing whether an expression is true or not.

It takes the following syntax:

! expression

It can also take the following syntax:

[! expression]

You can combine it with the "*if*" statement as shown below:

if test ! condition

then
1stcommand

2ndcommand

fi

Or

if [! condition]

then

1stcommand

2ndcommand

fi

If the expression is false it will return true. Consider the example shown below:

! −f name && exit

After running the above the command prompt will close if the file "*name*" is not found. In this case it doesn't exit since there is a file with the name.

"Continue" statement in shell

This statement is used in shell to resume an iteration of a FOR, WHILE or UNTIL loop enclosing. It takes a very simple syntax:

...

while true

do

[1stcondition] && continue

Command 1

Command 2

[2ndcondition] && break

done

...

The statement can also take the following syntax:

..

for j in thing

do

[condition] && continue

Command 1

Command 2

done

..

...

The following is an example of a MYSQL backup script that makes use of the "continue" statement:

#!/bin/bash

A script to backup mysql

run it while logged in as a root user

```bash
# Login information

MUSER="admin" # MySQL user name

MHOST="192.168.160.1"# MySQL server ip address

MPASS="password" # MySQL password

 # date format

NOW=$(date +"%d-%m-%Y")

 # path for the Backupfile

BACKUPPATH=/backup/mysql/$NOW
# create the backup path if it doesn't exist

[ ! -d $BACKUPPATH ] && mkdir -p $BACKUPPATH

 # obtain name lists from the database

DBS="$(/usr/bin/mysql -u $MUSER -h $MHOST -p$MPASS -Bse 'show databases')"
 for database in $DBS

do

# Backup the name of the file

FILE="${BPATH}/${database}.gz"

# if the name of the database is server or mint, then skip the
backup
```

```
[ "$database" == "server" ] && continue

[ "$database" == "mint" ] && continue

 # if okay, then we dump the database backup

  /usr/bin/mysqldump -u $MUSER -h $MHOST -p$MPASS
$database | /bin/gzip -9 > $FILE
done
```

Exit command

This command has the following syntax:

exit N

Chapter 14: Blockchain, Linux, and Net Neutrality

By now, you are probably beginning to see just how revolutionary blockchain is regarding how we use the Internet. This section will look at one of the most explosive political debates today: net neutrality.

When despots like Adolf Hitler, Josef Stalin, and Kim Jong-Il rose to power, one of their first moves was to control the spread of information. They systematically closed down any media outlets that spread dissenting views and centralized all information systems so that government-approved propaganda was all that the people heard. With the government determining what people can and can't listen to, it gave itself the ability to manipulate and distort the information that people heard. Many people came to believe that they had no alternative but to submit to their benevolent leaders.

Today, most people get their information through the Internet. The increasing centralization of the Internet's structure has made the manipulation of information easier, and many fear that it is well on its way to being used to brainwash people. One critical juncture on this pathway was the repeal of net neutrality.

Net neutrality refers to the ability of people to use different websites equally. It is a principle that Internet service providers have long been expected to adhere to, and many have defended it under the constitutional right of freedom of speech and freedom of the press.

The United States government looks at the Internet through the lens of its inception: with the client-server model. Most of its computers are run in this manner. In order to implement higher degrees of control over how people use the Internet, in December 2017 it voted to repeal net neutrality.

New legislation is requiring that ISPs apply the repeal of net neutrality to how they provide services to their customers. In practicality, this means that the speed of some websites is sped up, and the speed of others is drastically slowed down. Use of certain websites, while not illegal per se, can become so inconvenient and time-consuming that people might as well not be able to access them.

Blockchain and Linux both hold great potential in the fight against the repeal of net neutrality; this is just one reason why they work so well together. This chapter will conclude by exploring ways that the use of blockchain can guard net neutrality, in the face of a legal government that has officially repealed it.

Making the Internet open source. Linux and blockchains are both open-source softwares. The source codes can be accessed by anybody, and anybody can write changes into the code and submit them for approval. Together, they hold the potential to make the entire Internet an open-source software.

One means of doing that is through networks like Ethereum, Blockstack, and Lisk. The Linux ecosystem of distributions is so large and diverse that they can be used independently to create open-source Internets that the government is unable to censor. True, communist countries, like China and North Korea, have effectively blocked millions of websites, and North Korea has completely blocked the use of Linux. However, combining Linux with blockchain Internet models holds huge potential for fighting against the repeal of net neutrality.

How to attain such a feat is beyond the scope of this book series and is best suited for people who have a lot of experience in programming with both Linux and blockchain. However, it does remain a possibility.

Mesh nets. A mesh net is a means of providing Internet services through an indirect way rather than directly through the ISP. The way that it works is basically that a computer or other device connects to the ISP and becomes an Internet node. That device is then able to broadcast an Internet signal to other devices that are a part of the mesh network. It's not at all unlike using your phone as a portable hotspot so that other devices can access the Internet.

The use of mesh networks has been around for decades. Many blockchain enthusiasts see the repeal of net neutrality as the tipping point that will bring this old technology back into the limelight. Additionally, it will bring about a larger community to be a part of the blockchain network as people band together to fight against the repeal.

Projects are already underway to develop mesh nets using blockchain. They would enable users to bypass the net neutrality repeal by accessing the Internet via a blockchain that itself functions as a mesh net. Because no one is able to hack a blockchain, the government would be unable to censor the program.

Incorporating Linux into the development of an anti-net neutrality repeal mesh net would give the project even more potential in allowing people to continue to access the Internet freely. People would be able to continually use Linux to update the mesh net. Additionally, they would be able to encode their Linux computers to remain hidden from Internet censorship regulations.

Again, how to program this idea is far beyond the scope of this book series, but a group of savvy computer programmers could pull it off.

Blockchain as net neutrality. Additionally, some proponents of blockchain have shown that blockchian itself serves as a kind of net neutrality. Blockchain eliminates the need for a middle man to provide services, because it is able to execute all of its functions automatically. Networks like Ethereum and Lisk could effectively become the ISPs and sidestep any net neutrality laws. The open-source nature of Linux means that creating such a technology would be most feasible and compatible on a Linux-run computer.

Quantum computers. When quantum computers come onto the scene, they will have advanced cryptography that may actually be able to withstand government censorship, provided the right people are working on them. Some blockchains, like the tangle, are already working under protocols that would protect their cryptography even under quantum computing. The eventual use of quantum computers will be critical in the fight against net neutrality. Using Linux and blockchain now to create programs that will be compatible with them will help ensure that the fight ends favorably.

The Internet was originally designed in such a way that the spread of information could occur in a democratic, decentralized manner. Computers would be linked to each other in a co-equal network that would give no one computer dominance over another. Today, the reality is that the Internet has outgrown the client-server model. It has become heavily centralized, to the point that the United States government has made steps to censor and otherwise restrict its use. Blockchain and Linux both present alternatives to that model. Together, they represent a force that can overwhelm the government's best efforts at controlling the information that people have access to.

Hopefully by now, your appetite has been whetted to implement blockchain and its offshoots on your Linux device.

Blockchain and Linux

Blockchain and Linux seem to be made for each other. Together, they make the fight against the repeal of net neutrality stronger. They present a paradigm of decentralization and enabling anyone to write and implement code. They really are a match made in computer heaven.

Hyperledger

The Linux Foundation is behind the creation of Hyperledger, a massive blockchain enterprise that helps businesses implement blockchain technology in their corporate infrastructures. The Linux Foundation announced its creation in December 2015, and in February 2016 announced its charter members. The goal of Hyperledger is to improve accountability and transparency in businesses through blockchain. Technological giants, such as IBM and Intel, have gotten behind the project and contributed to its core software.

Private blockchains are controversial because they enable centralization. However, Hyperledger uses private blockchains, but they are not concentrated within any one business. For example, a bank that is part of the Hyperledger consortium does not get its own blockchain; it becomes part of a larger blockchain that encompasses multiple industries. The fact that other companies are part of the verification process and provide the immutability of data adds a layer of accountability onto the private blockchain. It doesn't become completely decentralized, but it is a few steps removed from complete centralization.

There are multiple Hyperledger blockchains and blockchain frameworks. For example, Hyperledger Fabric is a blockchain framework that enables companies to create decentralized applications, some of which their customers and clients can access from the front end. People are able to use it to create and execute smart contracts, thereby automating many of the companies' processes.

Hyperledger has been used across many different industries. It is used to track supply-chain shipping, meaning that it tracks the transit routes of goods that people eventually consume. Say that parents purchase a can of formula for their infant, and that batch is later found to have been contaminated. The parents will immediately want to know so that they can either not feed it to their baby or get their baby immediate medical treatment. Traditional technologies would alert them if there was found to be a problem, but use of Hyperledger enables them to actually scan the can of formula to track its entire transit route before buying it. It has also been used in maintaining health records and health insurance. It could be used to track things like car ownership so that people who buy used cars are able to find out exactly what the car in question has been through. The use of Hyperledger means that customers can be more confident in their purchases and the companies that they support.

The Hyperledger is open source, so in theory, anyone can access the source code and make improvements to it. Of course, those improvements must be approved by a 51% majority of nodes.

Hyperledger is written primarily in JavaScript, so any changes made will need to either be in JavaScript or need to be compiled from a different programming language (like Python or C++) into JavaScript.

Become a Blockchain Node

Becoming a node on Hyperledger requires permission, and that isn't likely to be granted unless you have high-level access inside a company that uses it. However, you can still set up your Linux computer to become a node on a public blockchain, like Bitcoin, Ethereum, Blockstack, or Lisk.

The first thing that you will need to do is decide which blockchain that you want to support. Different blockchains provide different benefits to nodes; for example, operators of Bitcoin nodes get access to the highest security wallets. Operating a node is not the same as operating a mine, so you won't get paid in cryptocurrency for your efforts. It really is a voluntary commitment that may give you some paybacks.

Turning your computer into a node is a huge commitment, one that will benefit the blockchain community through the dedication of your own resources. The second thing that you will need to do is make sure that your computer has enough memory on its hard drive to store the blockchain. Blockchains are huge, and as of the beginning of 2018, they can be as large as 50GB. Make sure that your computer has enough memory to accommodate the blockchain that you want to support.

The third thing that you will need to do is look closely at the core infrastructure of the blockchain that you want to support. While the blockchain itself is not complicated, the core infrastructure may be. For example, the Bitcoin Core is not particularly user friendly, and it may scare of potential new users. Make sure that you are up for the challenge, and if there is something about the core that you don't understand, find the answer.

You will want to keep a few other things in mind before turning your Linux computer into a node. One is that it will use a lot of Internet bandwidth (20GB a day). If you don't have an unlimited Internet plan, this could impede your ability to access the Internet for other things, like watching television or doing research for school. Another thing that you will need to keep in mind is that this computer will use up quite a bit of electricity. It won't use as much as a mine, but it will need to be running at full power six days a week. Finally, you need to be aware of the fact that running as a node will use a lot of your computer's resources. As a result, you may not be able to use your computer for other activities. The best course of action would be to use an older computer that you no longer use and connect it to a free energy supply (like solar). Doing so will enable you to contribute to your favorite blockchain community with the least drain on your own resources.

Once you have completed all of the above steps and you are aware of what operating a node entails, you need to download the core. If you are downloading Ethereum or a blockchain like it, you may need to download the specialized browser (like Mist) on which the blockchain runs. Be aware that because the core is such a large file, it can take a few hours and possibly even a few days to completely download. You may need to grant permission for the core to access the Internet; it is perfectly safe to do so.

Once the core is downloaded, you need to restart your computer. This will allow the core to integrate into your computer's resources and operate fully. Next, go to your Linux system's settings and enable the core to begin running whenever you start the computer. This process may vary depending on which Linux distribution you are using.

You will need to take care of the computer to ensure that it is running smoothly and carrying out its functions as a node as best as possible. Linux operating systems are not nearly as prone to viruses and other forms of malware as are other operating systems, so the risk of one impacting your ability to run as a node is pretty small. Still, you want to do a periodic check and restart your computer every few days.

Make sure that you are taking advantage of the benefits provided by running a node. And pat yourself on the back for helping blockchains remain strong and decentralized.

Become a Blockchain Miner

You can absolutely use a Linux OS to become a blockchain miner. Being a miner means that you will be able to earn virtual currency as a reward for your efforts! Before you get started, you need to decide which blockchain you want to mine for. Some of the most popular blockchains, especially Bitcoin and Ethereum, are so large that miners have to invest in expensive technology and continually upgrade their systems in order to remain competitive. Mining for them may not be profitable at all. Other blockchains, like DarkCoin and Lisk, have a hierarchy to determine who can mine. Do some research to decide which blockchain is the best one for you to mine for.

Keep in mind that mining is very energy intensive, and many people find that it is not profitable because their electric bills are so high. Before you start mining, make sure that you have a steady supply of cheap energy (such as solar) so that this doesn't happen. In addition to the cost of running your computer on high all the time, you will need to keep the computer cool, as mines frequently overheat. This can also contribute to a high electric bill.

This section will only focus on the software that you need in order to turn your computer into a mine. There is a lot of hardware that may be required in order to mine efficiently, but that is beyond the scope of this section.

Some blockchains have software specifically for Linux users to make mining easier and more profitable. For example Cgminer makes mining Bitcoin on Ubuntu much easier. Do some research and find out if the Linux distribution that you use has specialized mining software.

Download the necessary software to your computer. Keep in mind that tablets and even laptops aren't great for mining, unless the blockchain is relatively small (like Dogecoin or another altcoin). Also keep in mind that with Linux, many programs run better if you download the source code and then compile it. Doing this will actually enable you to make changes to the source code and make the software run even better!

You will also need to download the blockchain's core, just like if you were trying to turn your computer into a blockchain node. Once you have all of the necessary hardware, you can begin running the mining software and earning virtual currency!

Similarly to operating a node, your mining computer may drain so many resources that you aren't able to use it for much else. Unless you decide to build your own mine (a venture that some hard-core blockchain techies set out to do), you are probably best off using an older computer that you no longer use. Also, a mine will use a lot of energy and memory, so make sure that you have an ample supply of both. If you are unable to dedicate the necessary resources to running your own mine, consider joining a Linux-based mining pool. A mining pool is a group of miners who combine their computers' energy so that they can mine more efficiently. They then split the profits.

Linux and the Internet of Things (500 words)

With the rise of IOTA as the next generation in blockchain technology, there is plenty that needs to be said about Linux and the Internet of Things. Linux is actually the key component that makes the Internet of Things possible, as many of the gadgets that are a part of it are equipped with a postage-sized chip that uses Linux to connect to the Internet.

Linux's free distributions are behind many of the gadgets in the Internet of Things. Imagine that you are an entrepreneur with a great idea for programming a washing machine to be able to operate remotely. That way, people can time their loads of laundry so that they are finished just as they get home from work. You could go through all of the hassle of building a brand new network with your own technology that allows the washing machine to connect to the Internet and then to the user's smart phone. Or you could take an operating system that is already free and open source, and use that to program your washing machine. Without Linux, the creation of gadgets in the Internet of Things would be so high that it would be prohibitive. By the way, if you are using an Android phone to access your smart devices, you are using Linux because most Androids run on Linux.

Consider another important aspect of the Internet of Things: the Cloud. Your computer may have a very limited amount of memory and storage, but you can use it to access orders of magnitude of more memory through the Cloud. The Cloud is a critical part of the infrastructure of the Internet of Things, as it enables higher levels of access and power. The Cloud is also powered by Linux, which enables it to be integrated into the Internet of Things ecosystem.

The tangle, the third-generation blockchain technology, is essentially a feature of Linux. It can run on pretty much any operating system, but Linux makes up the bulk of the computational power of the Internet of Things. Without it, the tangle would be nothing more than a side interest of the super rich who have nothing better to do with their time.

The real question is why does all of this matter. It matters because Linux is powering the next generation of the Internet, and becoming a Linux programmer can put you on the cutting edge of these developments. It can even put you into a position in which you can make a lot of money.

In this chapter, you learned about Linux's relationship with blockchain technology and the growing Internet of Things. You are probably now seeing how crucial Linux is to developing the advanced gadgetry that is making many aspects of our lives easier.

Chapter 15: Build and Edit Applications

Once you have started to get the hang of writing and executing lines of code in the command line terminal, you can begin to build and edit applications. To edit an application, first download the raw source code (the procedure involved in doing this was explained in the first book in this series). Execute the program to ensure that everything is running smoothly and as the creator intended. Once you have gotten a feel for the program, you can think of how you might want to edit it to make it more customized to your own needs. Make sure that you keep a backup copy of the original code, just in case you aren't able to modify it as you like and end up with an error.

You can use the text editor to modify the source code. Isolate the area of code that you want to modify. Keep in mind that Python allows users to write comments, so it may be possible that the person who created the application clearly detailed in comments what each section does. This will make the process of finding which section you want to edit a lot easier.

Next, you can change the variables, parameters, functions, and other objects to customize the application. Maybe you have written a function that you have saved as a module, and you want to apply that function to the program. The module will be saved in the same format that we used to name the "Hello, World!" program: name.py. Let's say that you are creating a module that generates a sequence of prime numbers. You may want to name that moduleprime.py.

In order to access that module to use in editing a separate application, you follow the same process as when importing the "Hello, World!" program file into the command line terminal. Use the codeimport primeto import and execute the module within the application that you are working on. You can then apply a range; for example, say that you want to generate prime numbers all the way to 500. You could writerange(0,500)and immediately get those numbers executed.

When you are finished making edits to the application, run it in the command line terminal to see how it works. Does it do what you wanted it to do? Great! If not, go back and try again. Try to identify the particular coding sequence that is causing the error.

The best course of action is to start as small as possible. Don't try to change the graphics in a video game so that they are in 4D instead of 2D. Maybe you could start by writing macros files for your word processor (macros are functions that cause certain input variables to be replaced with certain output variables; for example, you could write a macro that causes the letter c to always be typed as an x). Once you start getting comfortable with making minor changes to existing applications, you can move up to more complex changes.

You may even get to the point where you are ready to begin building your own application! Remember that an application should be able to meet a particular need, either your own need or a need in the larger Linux community. Before you go through all of the trouble of building a new application, ask if your ideas can be carried out by modifying an existing application. If not, you can make a great contribution to the Linux community by building something brand new.

Start by building small pieces of your application at a time, and execute them at every step to ensure that they are running how you want them to run. When the whole thing is finished, you can submit the raw source code to the Linux community through forums like GitHub. You could even create your own blog with the source codes for the programs that you build!

Use an Integrated Development Environment

We already explored the process of using the command line terminal to write and execute code for Linux in Python. There is another option for doing this, and that is to use an Integrated Development Environment, or IDLE (you might could say that IDLE is a play on the fact that programmers tend to be lazy and are constantly looking for shortcuts). Ubuntu can be downloaded with a graphics IDLE, or you can download one separately. IDLE is written in Python, which makes it much easier to implement the code that you write.

IDLE is a great program for beginner coders to use for several reasons. One is that it automatically colors different syntax features in different colors, making finding mistakes much easier. For example, key words, text, and comments will all appear in different colors. Just like highlighting in your college textbooks made finding what you need to study much easier, color-coding these different features makes finding your mistakes much easier.

Another reason is because it uses a graphical user interface (GUI) instead of a command line interface. This makes it much more user friendly and easy to navigate.

When using IDLE, you don't necessarily need a text editor. You can write your code directly into IDLE, then execute it. If you are new to coding, you may want to consider using IDLE before moving on to the command line terminal.

IDLE does have a number of problems associated with it, so many programmers prefer to move on from it to the command line terminal as soon as possible.

Write Patches

As explained in the first book in this series, patches are changes made to the Linux kernel that improve it. This section will explain how to write a patch in Python and apply it to the kernel, which is written in C.

Keep in mind that there are many different methods to writing a patch. This is just one of them.

Diff is a command line program utilized by the Linux core development team. It compares the original source code with the changes that someone has proposed, and shows exactly what needs to be done to implement those changes. You need to keep the original source code for the particular area that you want to improve, and also write out the source code for your patch. You don't need to download a particular program; it is usually pre-packed with Linux operating systems. If you find that there is a problem in the execution of your code, you can compare your patch to the original source code using Diff to try to figure out where the problem is.

There are a few challenges that present themselves when you want to get started with writing a patch. The first is that the source code for the Linux kernel is 15 *million* lines long. You would have to be incredibly dedicated and disciplined in order to sit down and read through all of it! The thought of that much code may be so overwhelming that you don't even know where to start. The good news is that there are multiple points of entry for you to more easily find a specific location. Think of the points of entry like different entries in an encyclopedia or chapters in a book. You just have to find the right one and consider that your starting place.

Additionally, another good place to get started with finding your way through the 15 million lines of source code is to look for the overall data structures. If you are trying to map your way through a forest, you don't start by looking at the minute characteristics of individual trees. Instead, you start by trying to imagine a bird's eye view of the entire forest. In other words, you try to understand the overall structure (the data structure), and then you can figure out a path through the structure (the bits and pieces of the source code).

Another problem associated with getting started with the source code so that you can write a patch is the language. The kernel is written in C, but it is much more complicated than a standard C program. Reading the source code requires an advanced understanding of the C programming language. If you are not familiar with it, you may want to partner with somebody who is.

Nevertheless, you can write a patch using Python. Obviously, the first thing you will need to do is isolate the segment of code that you want to modify. Maybe there are multiple changes that you want to make. As explained in the last book, you should only write in one patch at a time. Once you have isolated the code, you will need to write out your changes. Again, your changes may be written in Python, while the source code is in C. We'll solve that problem in the next step.

Cython is a compiler that translates between Python and C, as well as some other programming languages. You can use it to translate your patch code so that it can be applied to the source code. Cython is also a programming language that allows for C-based extensions to Python; make sure that you download the compiler. Using the compiler to translate Python into C is probably the fastest and easiest way of getting the job done.

Once you have written in your patch, you want to test it out on your own computer. Run it in the command line terminal to see if it runs the way that you want it to run. The easiest way for your code to get rejected by the Linux core development team is for it to not work! Keep modifying it until it works exactly how you want it to work.

To date, over 12,000 programmers have contributed to the kernel. However, not all patches are accepted; in fact, most are not. If your patch is not accepted, there are still things that you can do make sure it is a contribution to the Linux community.

Implement it on your own computer. That's right. You can run the patched code on your own computer, even if it isn't part of the Linux kernel. If it makes your computer run more optimally, then it may be time to take some steps to share it with the world as an indie programmer.

Share it with friends. Do you know people who use Linux and might be interested in the patch that you made? Maybe you have some friends, programming cronies, or family members who are Linux enthusiasts (even if they are just getting started with Linux) and would be thrilled to have your patch applied to their computers.

Share it on forums. GitHub and Stack Overflow are just two forums that are frequented by members of the Linux community. There are so many Linux users who use forums that, if you share your patch through them, you will likely find plenty of people who want to implement it on their own computers. You will need to upload it as a .tar file so that others can download it and execute it.

And who knows? Your patch may become so ubiquitous that it ends up being accepted by the core development team as a part of the kernel after all!

If you are interested in learning more about the Linux kernel so that you can write patches, there are plenty of resources to help you find your way. The best resource is the connections that you will build with other Linux programmers on online forums and chat rooms. The Linux community is huge, and the people are often willing to help.

In this chapter, you learned a lot about how to apply your knowledge of Python to Linux so that you can start programming with it. You learned how to write some basic programs, like the "Hello, World!" program and execute it with the command line terminal. You also learned about IDLE, which you can use to begin with until you get more comfortable with coding. You learned how to edit source code for existing applications and even start building your own applications. Perhaps most importantly, you learned some of the basics for navigating the Linux kernel and writing a patch.

Conclusion

How you continue depends on what you want to do with your Linux distribution. For casual browsing and simple use, continue with Ubuntu and install the programs you need. For more adventurous people, consider installing a new distribution to see what each has to offer. Those wishing to learn even more deeply about Linux can install one such as Arch or DSL to build their own unique OS from scratch. Administrators and power users can install a server version of a distro to build their own Linux network, or they can consider changing over their environment from other operating systems to entirely free ones.

Conclusively, Linux is a powerful and relatively easy to use set of operating systems. But their real potential comes from the hard-to-master terminal and command line functions. Thank you for reading this publication, and I hope that it has shed some light on the mysterious subject of the defacto alternative operating system. If Linux has confused you or did not live up to expectations, I implore you to take a second look at the features it can offer. While it may not have the same caliber of games or 3rd party proprietary software, the OS is simple and customizable enough to be used as a primary OS with maybe Windows or OSX as a secondary OS. Alternatives exist for just about every program, so if it is possible to get rid of Microsoft and Apple entirely, it is highly recommended you do so. Thank you again, and make good use of your new Linux knowledge.

The next step is to start experimenting with the things in this book in order to see what crazy scripts you can come up with and how much you can automate your overall workflow!

www.ingramcontent.com/pod-product-compliance
Lightning Source LLC
LaVergne TN
LVHW051238050326
832903LV00028B/2457